PSYCHOANALYTIC RESPONSES
TO CHILDREN'S LITERATURE

PSYCHOANALYTIC RESPONSES TO CHILDREN'S LITERATURE

by Lucy Rollin *and* Mark I. West

McFarland & Company, Inc., Publishers
Jefferson, North Carolina, and London

PR
990
.R65
1999

British Library Cataloguing-in-Publication data are available

Library of Congress Cataloguing-in-Publication Data

Rollin, Lucy.
    Psychoanalytic responses to children's literature / by Lucy
Rollin and Mark I. West.
       p. cm.
    Includes bibliographical references and index.
    ISBN 0-7864-0674-7 (library binding : 50# alkaline paper) ∞
    1. Children's literature, English—History and criticism.
2. Children's literature—Illustrations—Psychological aspects.
3. Children's literature, American—History and criticism.
4. Children's literature—Psychological aspects. 5. Psychoanalysis
and literature. 6. Psychology in literature. 7. Psychology in
art. I. West, Mark I. II. Title.
PR990.R65   1999
820.9'9282'019—dc21   98-54256
                                                     CIP

Manufactured in the United States of America

McFarland & Company, Inc., Publishers
  Box 611, Jefferson, North Carolina 28640

For Malcolm Usrey,
our friend and colleague

ACKNOWLEDGMENTS

This book was written over a number of years in two different states on two incompatible computer systems, all of which made it difficult to pull it together into a unified manuscript. The person who helped the most in this daunting process was Karen McCraw. In addition to solving our complicated computer problems, she helped with all the details that go into producing a final manuscript. We appreciate her many contributions to this book.

We also wish to express our thanks to the other people who helped us in various ways, including Roger Rollin, Rodney Hunter, Robert A. Paul, M. Thomas Inge, Barbara Murphy, Joel West, and Nancy Northcott.

Some of the chapters in this book were previously published elsewhere in different forms and sometimes under different titles. Chapter 1 appeared in *Children's Literature in Education* 16, no. 4 (1985); Chapter 3 appeared in *South Carolina Review* 24, no. 1 (1991); Chapter 4 appeared in *Children's Literature* 18 (1990); Chapter 7 appeared in *Mind and Nature* 6 (1986); Chapter 8 appeared in *Children's Literature Association Quarterly* 15, no. 3 (1990); Chapter 10 appeared in *Children's Literature Association Quarterly* 19, no. 3 (1994); and Chapter 12 appeared in *University of Hartford Studies in Literature* 18, no. 1 (1986).

TABLE OF CONTENTS

Acknowledgments   vii

Preface   xi

Introduction   1

1—Regression and the Fragmentation of the Self in
       James and the Giant Peach—Mark I. West   17

2—The Mysterious and the Uncanny in *Nancy Drew*
       and *Harriet the Spy*—Lucy Rollin   23

3—Uncanny Mickey Mouse and His Domestication—
       Lucy Rollin   31

4—Narcissism in *The Wind in the Willows*—Mark I. West   45

5—The Reproduction of Mothering in *Charlotte's Web*—
       Lucy Rollin   53

6—Pinocchio's Journey from the Pleasure Principle to
       the Reality Principle—Mark I. West   65

7—Gazing and Mirroring in *The Prince and the Pauper*—
       Lucy Rollin   71

8—Childhood Fantasies and Frustrations in Maurice Sendak's
       Picture Books—Lucy Rollin   79

9—The Grotesque and the Taboo in Roald Dahl's Humorous
       Writings for Children—Mark I. West   91

10—Good-Enough Mother Hubbard—Lucy Rollin   97

11—Humpty Dumpty and the Anxieties of the Vulnerable
        Child—Lucy Rollin   111

12—Dream Imagery and the Portrayal of Childhood Anxieties
        in Nursery Rhyme Illustrations—Lucy Rollin   119

13—Repression and Rebellion in the Life and Works of
        Beatrix Potter—Mark I. West   129

14—Depictions of the Mother-Child Dyad in the Work of
        Mary Cassatt and Jessie Willcox Smith—Lucy Rollin   141

15—Guilt and Shame in Early American Children's Literature—
        Mark I. West   151

16—The Psychological Roots of Anthony Comstock's Campaign
        to Censor Dime Novels—Mark I. West   159

*Bibliography of Psychoanalytic Interpretations of
    Children's Literature*   171

Index   175

PREFACE

Children's literature has been our passion and our profession for years. We have, in our respective careers, explored many ways of talking and writing about it, but we have often found ourselves centered in an area which has not always been accessible to our students or even to some of our colleagues: psychoanalytic literary criticism. However, with the growing emphasis on theory in literary studies, this form of criticism has taken its place alongside other forms as an important contribution to literary interpretation. Despite its tendency to make readers uncomfortable, it offers insights into human nature, and hence into novels, plays, stories, and poems, which are unavailable without it. With this collection of essays, we bring together a number of basic psychoanalytic ideas that make this form of interpretation particularly appropriate for examining children's literature. In writing these essays, we have tried to avoid the mystifying jargon of some psychoanalytic criticism. On those occasions when we have used psychoanalytic terms, we have made an effort to define them first. Our aim is to make these essays understandable and interesting to a general audience.

In our introduction to the book, we have addressed four central questions:

> What is psychoanalysis, and why apply it to literature?
> What makes it especially congenial to use with children's literature?
> What problems with the theory might the novice have?
> What problems might a novice encounter in applying psychoanalytic theory?

In the course of this introduction we have tried to answer these questions fully, stressing the strengths of this form of literary criticism without

minimizing its weaknesses. While keeping the emphasis on classical analysis and Freud, we have tried to give a sense of the many revisions of the
theory.

We have organized the essays into two basic categories. The first seven
essays are psychoanalytic studies of characters from children's literature.
The rest apply psychoanalytic theory to other aspects of children's literature, such as readers' responses to children's books, the illustrations that
accompany many children's books, or the cultural milieu that surrounds all
forms of literature. At the end of this book, we have supplied a bibliography of works of psychoanalytic criticism that deal with children's literature. We hope these essays communicate our abiding fascination with
children's literature, our love of it, and its endless possibilities for all kinds
of interpretation.

INTRODUCTION

"There is always another story, one we haven't necessarily bargained for."
—Adam Phillips, *On Flirtation*

Some children once wrote to Lewis Carroll and asked him to explain the meaning behind his poem *The Hunting of the Snark*. In his reply, he said he "meant nonsense," but added, "Still, you know, words mean more than we mean to express when we use them: so a whole book ought to mean a great deal more than the writer meant" (Cohen 409). Leaving aside Carroll's joke that more words "ought to" make more meaning, his comment about the work surpassing the intent of the writer is the foundation for all literary interpretation. When we explore a literary work, we, too, believe it is more than words on the page. There are insights into human thought and feeling that can enlarge our lives. The intent of psychoanalytic literary criticism and interpretation is to discover more about the work and about ourselves, to experience the freedom that comes with understanding, but to realize that there will always be more than we can know. There will always be the "story we hadn't bargained for."

When Freud listened with hovering attention to his patients' words, he believed there was more meaning in them than they meant to express. When he wrote down his own dreams, when he heard jokes and slips of the tongue in everyday conversations, he looked for more meaning, pursuing it into the darkest corners. Sometimes, his discoveries and his interpretations freed his patients from their crippling neuroses and made them once again able to love and to work. This, Freud said, was the intent of psychoanalysis. For psychoanalysis is first and foremost a therapy, designed to

1

help those who suffer from neurotic symptoms which are severe enough to prevent them from enjoying their lives. As a therapy it is practiced in this country most frequently by medical doctors who have taken analytic training as an addition to their medical studies, but in Europe it may be practiced by those without medical degrees.

However, as it is a therapy of the human heart and mind, it has become much more than a form of medicine. Because it suggests that human beings are often in conflict with their societies, their friends and families, and with themselves, and that the causes of this conflict may be buried in unconscious or unremembered events and wishes, psychoanalysis has become something closer to a philosophy (some even say a religion). It offers a particular way of looking at human life, a lens through which we may focus on human thought, behavior, and language, and gain insights into what makes us able to love, work, and live peacefully (or not so peacefully) with our fellow human beings. Whether or not we engage in actual therapy, the concepts of psychoanalysis teach us to see ourselves anew—at times suffering and conflicted, at other times grandiose and deluded, but always as complex, multidimensional human beings capable of remarkable generosity, strength, and joy.

Literature does the same thing. Whether we read *King Lear* or *Charlotte's Web*, a poem by Wordsworth or one by Nikki Giovanni, we see human life as richer, more densely marked by deeper sorrows and greater happiness, than we did before. Like psychoanalysis, literature opens a window onto human life that enriches readers beyond what they might conceive of by themselves. This is why we read and why we encourage children to read.

It is also why the founder of psychoanalysis, Sigmund Freud, credited poets, novelists, and playwrights with the real discovery of psychoanalysis. Both psychoanalysis and literature encourage us to think beyond the surface of language and to explore its various possible meanings. Freud, who began his career as a neurologist, first considered the possibility of such hidden meanings when he discussed the case of "Anna O." with his colleague Joseph Breuer. "Anna O." was Breuer's patient, whom he was treating with hypnosis. Her symptoms—a nervous cough, squinting, hallucinations, and an inability to drink water—remained until she began to describe her hallucinations. After describing them, she found she was able to recall events in her early life that troubled her, and at that point her symptoms dramatically lessened or disappeared. She called this method "the talking cure," or "chimney sweeping." But as she became very dependent on Breuer and developed other symptoms, it was Freud who encouraged his reluctant colleague to understand the deeper roots of this patient's troubles (her sexual attraction to Breuer), and who began to try this "talking" cure on other patients, without the aid of hypnosis and with startling success. He developed the skill of listening into an art. His patience and his intuitive skills led him into the depths of human pain and confusion. He gave his technique a form and a vocabulary, and thus psychoanalysis became an interpretive strategy, just as literary criticism has its vocabulary and is an interpretive strategy.

Freud always gave credit to his early patients for showing him the technique of listening with what he termed "hovering attention," the basics of which were in place by 1892. But in 1850 Nathaniel Hawthorne described it vividly in *The Scarlet Letter*: if a doctor is intelligent, intuitive, and able to keep himself in the background, if he can receive a patient's confidences "without tumult" and mostly in silence, with only a word or two at times to show that he understands, "—then, at some inevitable moment, will the soul of the sufferer be dissolved, and flow forth in a dark, but transparent stream, bringing all its mysteries into the daylight" (1051). This is the analytic attitude: the ability to listen, to wait, to be alert for patterns as they reveal themselves, and only then to interpret. The best analysts, and the best literary critics, do just that.

Freud loved literature. His works are full of references to Homer, Sophocles, Goethe, Shakespeare, Milton, Schiller, Ibsen, E.T.A. Hoffmann, Kafka, and many others less well-known today. In 1906 he was asked on a questionnaire to list "ten good books." His list and his accompanying comments show the remarkable variety of his reading and of his taste in authors, languages, and subjects; in addition to books by Anatole France and Emile Zola, he particularly liked Kipling's *Jungle Book* and Mark Twain's *Sketches*. He defined good books in the same way that a young lover of Betsy Byars' stories might today: they are "books to which one stands in rather the same relationship as to 'good' friends, to whom one owes a part of one's knowledge of life and view of the world" (Gay, *Freud Reader* 540).

Perhaps this deep and unaffected love of books is one reason he was such a fine storyteller himself. It may also be one reason that psychoanalysis itself so closely resembles literature as well as the interpretation of it. Freud's case history of the young lawyer who came to be called the "Rat Man" resembles a mystery tale in its piling up of clues and suspense. His description of the rich young Russian whom he called the "Wolf Man" traces the story of a neurosis evolving from a childhood dream of white wolves sitting in a tree, and is accompanied by the patient's own drawing of this dream (Gay, *Freud Reader* 405). Freud's most famous and controversial case history, "Dora," has the drama and family intrigue of an 18th century novel. And he is as much a poet as a narrative artist, creating vivid similes and metaphors for abstract concepts. Uncovering memories and fears from childhood is like uncovering an ancient and buried city. The ego is like a walled city, beleaguered by the forces of the id. The work of the psyche to control the id and allow the ego to function is reclamation work, like draining the Zuider Zee.

Freud's reliance on narrative and poetic language bothers some critics of psychoanalysis, particularly analyst Donald Spence, who believes that these literary methods offer a false sense of closure and truth in the psychoanalytic setting. In his 1907 essay "Creative Writers and Daydreaming," Freud did in fact take an apparently narrow view of literature as merely therapy for the artist's neuroses. But his natural, thoughtful, wide-ranging engagement with literature, as it permeates the entire sweep of his work, testifies to his ultimate view of the plasticity of the imagination. We may, as interpreters of literature, accept it as one way—perhaps the best way—of speaking the unspeakable about the human heart.

For a variety of reasons, psychoanalytic criticism is especially congenial to *children's* literature. Freud was, of course, fascinated by children. He believed that the dreams and play of normal children, and the neuroses of troubled ones, opened a window onto adult conflicts. He believed, using his archeological metaphor, that our childhood wishes and fantasies remained buried beneath our adult choices and attitudes, affecting them when we least knew it, as in the case of the "Wolf Man." One of his famous case histories is of "Little Hans," a five-year-old boy who suddenly developed a fear of horses. At the request of the parents, over a period of weeks Freud listened attentively to the boy's anxious descriptions of his fears, watching as he punched his father and then kissed the place he had hit. He gradually and gently interpreted to the boy that perhaps the horses represented his father. As these interpretations "took hold," Hans' phobia receded, and he ultimately grew into a healthy, productive opera director (Gay, *Life* 258–60).

Freud was also a proud and loving father, although less demonstrative—as was appropriate for his time and culture—than we prefer today. His son Martin described an incident when he was humiliated on the skating rink and felt somehow permanently disgraced; at home, his father, seeing his depression and embarrassment, invited Martin into his study and asked him to describe the incident. Martin could not remember what his father said to him, but afterward, the incident lost its tragic quality and became a "trifle" (Gay, *Life* 161–2).

The solution to one of Freud's most puzzling theoretical problems was suggested to him partly by his grandchild. According to his theory of dreams, most dreaming was wish-fulfilling and pleasant, bringing a measure of relief, conscious or unconscious, to the dreamer. However, how could he account for the disturbing dreams of, for example, war veterans, in whose dreams their most terrifying moments in battle recurred time and again? One day he noticed that his eighteen-month-old grandson, who was much attached to his mother, never cried when she left him, but instead played a game by himself. Ernst took a wooden spool tied to his crib with string, and threw it over the side, out of his sight, saying to himself "O-o-o-o," which the family took to mean *fort*, the German word for "gone." He would then pull the string, bringing the spool back into his view, and cry happily, "*Da!*"—the German word for "there." Freud speculated that the boy was learning by repetition to master his distress at his mother's disappearance; the more he symbolically repeated her departure and her return, the more he could control his feelings. Just so, Freud reasoned, the repetition of anxiety dreams might allow the dreamer eventual mastery of the fearsome situation that gave rise to them. As he did further research and thinking, he came to believe this explanation was the most useful one and described his conclusions in 1920 in *Beyond the Pleasure Principle*. This "*fort/da*" game has become the most famous children's game in psychoanalytic literature.

One of the most difficult areas of Freudian theory for the novice is its emphasis on sexuality. Freud's frank and insightful discussions of sex, and his theory of the evolution of human sexual desires, broke new ground in its own day and at times distressed even his colleagues. It was the sexual attraction "Anna O." felt for Breuer which Freud addressed in his discussions with his colleague and which Breuer found difficult to admit at the time, although he later acknowledged its truth. Most bothersome was, and is, Freud's belief that our sexual natures are formed early in childhood, and that children themselves experience sexual feelings. This is an idea which many find repugnant and which causes some to reject psychoanalysis out of hand. It is also responsible for some of the funniest parodies of psychoanalytic literary criticism, especially Frederick Crews' mock analysis of *Winnie-the-Pooh* in his clever spoof of all literary criticism, *The Pooh Perplex* (1963). Crews has his imaginary analyst, "Dr. Karl Anschauung," conclude that A. A. Milne is a "relatively simple" case of advanced animal-phobia and obsessional defense; somewhat complicated by anal-sadistic and oral-helpful fantasies, skoptophilia and secondary exhibitionism, latently homosexual trends in identification with the mother, severe castration anxiety and compensatory assertiveness, and persistence of infantile misconstructions of birth, intercourse, and excrement (136). Crews wrote a classic psychoanalytic biography of Hawthorne; only one who knows psychoanalytic criticism extremely well could skewer it with such hilarious accuracy.

Certainly infantile sexuality is a key concept in psychoanalytic thinking. But in Freudian theory, the notion of sexuality is much more general than we usually think of it today. The term covers all sorts of pleasant bodily feelings, not just those of the sexually active adult. Freud said that children's feelings are "polymorphous," having many forms and affecting many areas of the body—most of our skin, for example. Such feelings tend to become more localized in adults, but they do not disappear, and remain responsible for much human happiness—as well as human bewilderment, anxiety, and suffering, especially when they come into conflict with society's controls on our behavior. One of the most powerful areas of psychoanalysis for the literary critic is just this, for most *literature* acknowledges that we are body as well as mind and spirit; but some literary *criticism*, in its arid intellectualism, implies that we are cerebellum only. Freud has given us a way to acknowledge the whole person, and a vocabulary to show some of the ways the child lives on in the adult. The same linkage creates children's literature: it is written by adults who call on their memories and experiences—physical and emotional—from childhood and bring them alive again for child readers, who then respond to those correspondences in their own thoughts and feelings.

One of Freud's most famous comments, made in response to those who thought he was finding too many sexual symbols in everything, was, "Sometimes a cigar is just a cigar." Today, psychoanalysis is *not* just psychoanalysis. The beginning reader and writer in this field may feel bewildered by the many varieties of psychoanalytic theory and the literary applications of it. As with any theory, psychoanalysis has had many critics and undergone multiple revisions, from the time Freud first began publishing his clinical findings and advancing his iconoclastic ideas; but this scrutiny has generally encouraged a strengthening and refinement of Freudian thought. Generally, literary critics make clear, early on in their books or essays, which variation of psychoanalytic theory they are applying, and readers need to be alert to this information. In the following paragraphs, we offer some basic characteristics of a few major critiques and revisions.

Freud's daughter Anna, his youngest child and the only one of his children to take up analysis as a profession, was among the first to shift the emphasis of her father's theories. Whereas he analyzed the unconscious forces which pushed or insinuated themselves into daily life, usually to our shame or regret, Anna Freud analyzed the defenses that we erect against those forces. For her, the whole aim of psychoanalysis was to restore the ego to healthy functioning. To achieve that end, she examined the range of ways, both conscious and unconscious, that we use to protect ourselves from unpleasant thoughts and desires. Her methods, practiced today by many analysts, have come to be called ego psychology, and have given us the famous term "defense mechanism."

Other female contemporaries and colleagues expressed considerable discomfort with Freud's resolutely patriarchal attitudes. These—which he shared with most men of his time and culture—led him to emphasize the child's relationship with the father over that with the mother, expressing the idea that the female superego was underdeveloped; to use the boy's sexual development as the "normal" model and the girl's as problem-plagued; and finally to ask that famous and despairing question, "What do women want?" Melanie Klein, in her revisions of Freudian theory, shifted the emphasis to the child's earliest relationship—with the mother. Karen Horney took exception to Freud's concept of penis envy and suggested that boys may envy girls' child-bearing capacities as well. More recently, Carol Gilligan's studies of adolescent girls show that girls' moral concepts develop along different but no less personally effective lines than boys'; society, however, still privileges the hierarchical, male model of moral development. Juliet Mitchell's book *Psycho-Analysis and Feminism* (1974) surveys this entire field of patriarchy in analytic thought, both Freud's and others', with remarkable thoughtfulness.

Some have reconsidered Freudian psychoanalysis on other grounds. Carl Jung, one of Freud's earliest colleagues and one of the first to leave Freud's circle to establish himself as an independent thinker, radically revised one of Freud's essential notions: that of the individual unconscious. Jung came to believe that the unconscious was a kind of world, filled with myths, ideas, and symbols which each individual shares with the surrounding culture. He added a spiritual and cultural element to his psychoanalysis which many have missed in Freud. Erik Erikson, whose biography of Martin Luther is his most famous contribution to psychoanalytic interpretation, translated Freud's ideas of fluid psychosexual stages of development into a series of psychosocial crises that we go through to achieve autonomy and identity; an orderly sequence of conflicts between individual and society which grows progressively more complex, but remains basically the same for everyone. His theories have been widely summarized, in very abbreviated form, in children's literature textbooks for teachers, usually alongside Abraham Maslow's hierarchy of needs and Jean Piaget's cognitive development scheme. They have become generally more useful in pedagogy than in literary interpretation, but Murray Schwartz has recently lauded Erikson for bringing new insights to the interpretation of dreams, and hence to literary interpretation.

The theories of D. W. Winnicott were very influential in psycho-analysis and have now permeated a great deal of psychoanalytic literary interpretation. Winnicott was a British pediatrician who became interested in psychoanalysis when he encountered Melanie Klein's ideas. In his profession, he daily watched children with their mothers, and came to believe, with Klein, that this relationship was central to human life and imagination. His way of practicing analysis, with children and with adults, was to encourage them to be playful and to acknowledge their need for acceptance and closeness with another human being. As he observed children with their dolls, blankets, and teddy bears, he theorized that this beloved, but often ill-treated, object represented the mother-figure—not so much the real, human mother but a kind of symbolic construction of her in the child's mind. The purpose of this "transitional object," as he called it, was to allow the child gradually to give up its dependence on the mother-figure.

One of his most important contributions to psychoanalytic theory was his concept of play. He imagined a space between baby and mother, when they were truly and naturally playing, which was neither entirely real nor entirely imaginary and where they relaxed and trusted each other; he called it "potential space," and believed that here, the baby came to con-ceive of the world, itself, and the mother symbolically—a step necessary to healthy maturation. He saw art, fiction, poetry, theater, and religious ritual as this kind of play for adults, neither subjective nor objective, nei-ther "inside" nor "outside," but something else, and something essential for psychological health.

By far the most influential figure in American psychoanalytic literary criticism today is the French analyst Jacques Lacan. He rose to prominence in 1950s Paris but immediately became a target for controversy with his unorthodox approach to the analytic session with patients. He broke from the official psychoanalytic community in France and established his own psychoanalytic school there in 1963. His writing is deliberately obscure and difficult (he wanted as nearly as possible to recreate the chaos and mystery of the unconscious), and despite his claims that he was adhering to basic Freudian theory, he rewrote and reconfigured the entire Freudian system until it often seems quite new. His most significant contribution to mod-ern psychoanalysis is his emphasis on language. He reminds us that language *is* the analytic encounter; without language there is no psychoanalysis. But language is always unreliable, only a tissue of symbols, hiding the unconscious even as it pretends to reveal it. Along with these ideas, Lacan's description of a mirror stage in young children, and of the early emergence of desire as a fundamental part of human life, are rich with possibility for interpreting children's literature. Much recent Lacanian literary criticism, heavily dependent on his obscure jargon and his French abbreviations, ends in a barrage of abstractions that seem unconnected to the text it supposedly treats. However, in a chapter of *The Nimble Reader: Literary Theory and Children's Literature* (1996), Rod McGillis shows that we may achieve a sensitive and cogent Lacanian reading (in this case of a Victorian *Little Red Riding Hood*) without stretching it on the rack of Lacanian theory.

In addition to the many varieties of psychoanalytic theory, and certainly troublesome—and troubling—to any reader/writer in this area, are the attacks on Freud himself which have recently appeared in the academic and popular presses; these generally come from academics and social scientists and occasionally from those in the medical profession. On the one hand, they accuse Freud of being arrogant and deluded, and hence deluding all his followers. For example, Freud called psychoanalysis a science, and tried to describe it in scientific terms, when it is clearly not a science. It cannot participate in strict scientific method; its truths are incapable of proof. Moreover, it is sometimes a failure as a therapy—even Freud's patients often were not "cured"—and has been superseded by shorter, less expensive therapies, such as meditation or short-term counseling. Analysts generally counter these arguments by pointing out that Freud's use of scientific terminology was in keeping with his early professional life as a neurologist and anatomist of the brain; it was natural to turn to it when he wanted acceptance in the scientific community of his day for his radically new ideas. But they assert that the clinical validity of the method stands on its own, and that analysis does work as a therapy, not as easily or quickly as other therapies but more thoroughly over time.

In the early 1980s a more serious issue arose regarding Freud's early assumption that all adult neuroses were caused by sexual abuse in childhood. Freud had found so many references to it in his patients that he believed for a short time that it must be true. However, he soon abandoned this concept (usually now called "the seduction theory") in favor of the idea that many of the seductions described by neurotics were fantasies springing from the child's early and unconscious attraction to the parent.

This kind of fantasy was the groundwork for the theory of the Oedipus complex. With the increasing legal and media attention today being given to incidents of child abuse, and the public sense that the practice has become more frequent, Freud's shift in theory now appears to some to be a cover-up—willful or deluded, but dangerous either way. The issue remains unsettled. However, it seems that although Freud did not claim that there was *never* seduction or abuse involved in adult neuroses, he, and perhaps many analysts since, may have finally underestimated its frequency.

Freud has also been taken to task for his early advocacy of cocaine as a pain-killer and stimulant. He tried it himself, and wrote a paper praising its usefulness in relieving morphine addiction. Freud was not the only scientist to praise, use, or advocate the drug; its addictive properties had not yet come to light. Freud later deeply regretted his early involvement with it; Freud's biographer Peter Gay calls it "one of the most troubling episodes in Freud's life" (45). But as with the "seduction theory," today's media attention to drugs supplies a perspective on this issue different from that of Freud and his contemporaries.

Another troubling episode was Freud's friendship with Wilhelm Fliess, an ear, nose, and throat specialist with excellent credentials and a fine reputation at the time. His theories about the nose as the governing organ of the body and his strange numerological system of proof now appear to be quackery, and Freud's intense friendship with and respect for him an aberration. Freud allowed Fliess to operate on the nose of one of his patients, and then discovered to his horror that Fliess had left a large amount of gauze in her nose; the resultant bleeding put her life briefly at risk. Freud eventually gave up his friendship with the man, but critics of Freud see this strange relationship as evidence of Freud's credulity; he believed in the strange ideas of others just as he believed in his own. And some even assert that Freud had an affair with his wife's sister, Minna Bernays.

Much of the evidence for such charges comes from Freud's voluminous correspondence, which many have read with great attention, dissection, and analysis. But there is much about Freud, too, in the Freud Archives in the Library of Congress, that will not be available to scholars until the year 2102. What effect more knowledge about Freud will have on psychoanalysis itself remains to be seen. Meanwhile, the number of angry books and articles, generated by some scholars and critics of Freud's failings as a person and as a professional—his ambition, his arrogance, his struggles as he worked through his new ideas—often seems out of proportion, as if they feel betrayed that psychoanalysis has not lived up to its promise of an ultimate truth about human life, or that its founder was an imperfect person.

Frederick Crews, whose psychoanalytic biography of Hawthorne is a classic in the field, now believes that psychoanalysis is a "collective contagious delusional system" (Winkler 6); he has become the most eloquent spokesman for this disillusionment. But, so far the effects of these charges on the application of psychoanalytic theory to literature have been negligible. The theory has increasingly become part of intellectual history and language, and, as a political scientist has commented, "what works in medicine and what works in scholarship are really two separate issues. Leaving aside the question of its clinical worth, psychoanalysis is a very effective interpretive tool" (Winkler 6).

So how do we learn to use this interpretive tool? In 1910, Freud was very concerned about what he called "wild" analysis: the tendency of some doctors to apply psychoanalytic theory in a cursory or hasty way, without adequate knowledge or preparation (a problem that always plagues new medical techniques and theories). He worried about the integrity of his profession, and about the health of patients in such situations. The scholar applying psychoanalytic theories to literature does not endanger a suffering human mind in the same way as "wild" analysis might in the consulting room, but like analysts we must aim to be gentle and informed. We must try to allow the literary work its "life," its integrity as an artistic entity. And although any theoretical lens will emphasize some qualities over others, we hope not to distort the work, and above all not to rob it of the beauty which attracts us to it in the first place.

One annoying difficulty in applied psychoanalysis is its terminology. All theories have their jargon, but psychoanalytic terms are unusually tricky because they are a combination of German, Latin, and now French constructions along with their English translations. Freud's early translators often chose Latin words for Freud's German terms, probably because they sounded more scientific and medical. But Freud was very aware of language and chose his words carefully. When we say *id*, *ego*, and *superego*, we miss the natural, human connotation that Freud wanted when he chose the everyday German words *das Es*, *Ich*, and *Über-Ich*—literally, "the It," "I" or "me," and "super-me." The idea of *drives* is an important one in psychoanalysis. It means something like "instinct" but it has a mechanical connotation. Freud's German word for it was *Trieb*, which refers to something more biological, more like a small plant forcing its way through stone. And of course Lacan offered a whole new system of terms in French *and* English: *jouissance*, *petit à*, and the Symbolic Order, for example. The novice reader and writer in the field cannot be aware of many such subtleties, but can try to understand the chosen terms as well as possible and to define them in the context of the literary interpretation. Charles Rycroft's *A Critical Dictionary of Psychoanalysis* can be very helpful as a reference. Courage and homework are essential, but so is remembering that the terms are describing *human* emotions or characteristics, most of them pretty ordinary, for all their esoteric or impersonal sounds.

A more subtle, difficult problem is remembering what is being analyzed. There are several options for interpreting a literary work, no matter what theory we are applying. We may focus on a particular character, such as Heidi, or Pinocchio. What may we learn about real human beings from this fictional person? We may focus on the author, placing the work in the context of his or her life to see what we may learn about the individual creative mind—its interests, fantasies, habits, and development. We may, as Lacanian theory has shown us, focus on the language of the work itself—its metaphors, rhythms, textures. What messages does it send that might allow us to learn something more than what it says on the surface? We may use the work to analyze the reader, either ourselves or some specific reader or group of readers whom the author had in mind. We may in some cases use the work to explicate a particular psychoanalytic concept.

On the other hand, Norman Holland's experiments in reader response theory suggest that we all read literature selectively, unconsciously projecting our own fantasies into it and reshaping it to suit our individual identities. He explains why most of us have at some time been amazed when a friend reads the same book we read but comes up with an entirely different interpretation. He shows us that a work of literature can so easily blend with our own mental images that we cannot tell them apart. Psychoanalytic literary criticism, because it focuses on unconscious conflicts and fantasies, is especially prone to such confusions. No doubt, most of the essays in this book tell at least as much about their authors as about their subjects, probably without our knowing it.

This personalizing opportunity is, however, one of the strengths of psychoanalytic literary criticism. If we acknowledge our personal involvement openly; if we make clear the choices we have made and why we have made them, we have an opportunity to bring ourselves to a poem, story, or play more completely than other theoretical systems allow. In the nineteenth century, literary criticism allowed the writer's voice a strong presence. For many years this voice was hidden under various theoretical maneuvers, making the criticism seem to exist impersonally, in the heady air of pure intellect. Some of the essays in this book, written a few years earlier, partake of this tradition. But psychoanalytic criticism today is returning the critic to the criticism, the interpreter to the interpretation, without abandoning sound theoretical principles. All literary criticism stretches toward this ideal.

The most serious, and most valid, complaint about psychoanalytic literary criticism is that it too often ignores historical and cultural context. It behaves, some say, as if human emotions exist in a vacuum, as if they are not affected by time or place. Even if they don't say so, psychoanalytic critics apparently believe a neurosis is a neurosis, dream mechanisms are the same for everyone, the Oedipus complex exists in every culture, and so on. Freud, as he developed and refined his ideas and aimed for a kind of scientific purity, was nonetheless a product of his time and culture; psychoanalysis can seem infused with his political and moral attitudes—such as the dominance of the father in the family triad.

One of the great values of all the revisions of Freud—Jung's, Klein's, Winnicott's, Lacan's, and all the others—is that they allow us to see this weakness in Freudian psychoanalysis and begin to make corrections for it. We should also be aware of different ways of looking at literature other than psychoanalytically. The Marxist approach to literature, while it may seem quite opposite from and inimical to the psychoanalytic approach, is similar in a fundamental way: both theories believe that human freedom and independence are illusory. The psychoanalyst focuses on the internal conflicts that control us unconsciously—repressed childhood trauma, aggression, sexual desire. The Marxist focuses on the social systems that control our lives in a given time in history, systems so well entrenched that we accept them unthinkingly as part of everyday reality—the emphasis in capitalist societies on "free enterprise" and profit, for example. Marxist critics Jack Zipes and Ian Wojcik-Andrews have trained this lens on children's literature and shown us, for example, that the story of *Little Red Riding Hood* has been rewritten countless times to reflect changing societal attitudes toward girls, or that a children's "classic" is more a product of a societal power structure than of an individual creative mind. Anthropology too can dramatically enlarge our image of ourselves, especially when the subject is material from folklore. Cultural anthropologist Alan Dundes is especially good at tempering psychoanalytic interpretations of folklore with a strong emphasis on how various cultures shift meaning and emphasis in a given tale, such as "Cinderella." Working alongside psychoanalysis, these theoretical strategies offer a picture of human life more complete than each offers alone.

Finally, as the previously quoted passage from *The Pooh Perplex* shows, psychoanalytic interpretation can seem merely humorous, or even ridiculous, just as any theoretical concept does when the jargon takes over. Another reason it seems funny is that its references to sex and the body can make us uncomfortable, so we laugh, as we do at a risqué joke, to cover our embarrassment; or in surprise and relief at being able to say or think such things in polite company. This quality is exacerbated when the critic is full of high seriousness, apparently insisting on the correctness of his or her interpretations. Bruno Bettelheim's classic work on fairy tales, *The Uses of Enchantment*, sometimes unfortunately adopts this tone. At these times the "fit" between the topic—attitudes toward excrement, for example— and the tone begins to seem awkward, forced, or even silly. However, a light touch, a sense of humor, and an open mind can help the literary critic to minimize this difficulty. Some jargon is inevitable, of course, but we can try not to rely on it too much. We should remember as well that while the analogy between psychoanalysis and literary criticism is close—both probe for "hidden" meanings in human language and emotion—it is far from exact. A literary work, whether it is *Charlotte's Web* or Poe's *Annabel Lee*, is a human utterance full of feeling and significance, but it is not the chaotic free association of an analysand speaking to an analyst; it is not a confused and suffering human being requesting therapy. We may take the literary text seriously without placing excessive burdens on it.

Our epigraph about the story we didn't bargain for comes from Adam Philips' book *On Flirtation: Psychoanalytic Essays on the Uncommitted Life* (1994). Phillips, a child psychotherapist in London, likes the idea of flirtation. It suggests possibilities, keeps the future open. It is a "game of taking chances, of plotting illicit possibilities" (xiv). It is experiment, curiosity, irreverence. But, Phillips points out, we only flirt with serious things. In this book, we invite you to flirt with psychoanalytic ideas in children's literature. We take them seriously, but, we hope, not too seriously. We hope you will be inspired to find a story of your own that you didn't bargain for.

Works Cited

Bettelheim, Bruno. *The Uses of Enchantment.* New York: Alfred A. Knopf, 1976.
Bowie, Malcolm. *Lacan.* Cambridge, MA: Harvard University Press, 1991.
Children's Literature 18 (1990), 125–143.
Cohen, Morton. *Lewis Carroll: A Biography.* New York: Alfred A. Knopf, 1995.
Crews, Frederick. *The Pooh Perplex.* New York: E. P. Dutton, 1963.
_____. *The Sins of the Fathers.* New York: Oxford University Press, 1966.
_____. *Skeptical Engagements.* New York: Oxford University Press, 1986.
Dundes, Allen. *Cinderella: A Casebook.* New York: Wildman Press, 1983.
Erikson, Erik. *The Young Man Luther: A Study in Psychoanalysis and History.* New York: Norton, 1958.
Gay, Peter. *Freud: A Life for Our Time.* New York: W. W. Norton, 1988.
_____, ed. *The Freud Reader.* New York: W. W. Norton, 1989.
Gilligan, Carol. *In a Different Voice.* Cambridge, MA: Harvard University Press, 1982.

Hawthorne, Nathaniel. *The Scarlet Letter.* In *The Norton Anthology of American Literature Vol. 1* (1979).

Holland, Norman. *Dynamics of Literary Response.* New York: Oxford University Press, 1968.

Horney, Karen. *Feminine Psychology.* New York: W. W. Norton, 1967.

Jung, Carl Gustav. *Man and His Symbols.* Garden City, NY: Doubleday, 1964.

Klein, Melanie. *Love, Guilt, and Reparation, and Other Works 1921–1945.* London: Hogarth Press, 1975.

Malcolm, Janet. *In the Freud Archives.* New York: Alfred A. Knopf, 1984.

McGillis, Roderick. *The Nimble Reader: Literary Theory and Children's Literature.* New York: Twayne, 1996.

Mitchell, Juliet. *Psycho-Analysis and Feminism.* New York: Vintage Books, 1975.

Phillips, Adam. *On Flirtation: Psychoanalytic Essays on the Uncommitted Life.* Cambridge, MA: Harvard University Press, 1994.

Phillips, Jerry, and Ian Wojcik-Andrews. "Notes Toward a Marxist Critical Practice." *Children's Literature* 18 (1990): 127–130.

Rycroft, Charles. *A Critical Dictionary of Psychoanalysis, New Edition.* London: Penguin Books, 1995.

Schwartz, Murray M. "Where Is Literature?" In *Transitional Objects and Potential Spaces.* Ed. Peter L. Rudnytsky. New York: Columbia University Press, 1993.

Spence, Donald. *The Freudian Metaphor.* New York: W. W. Norton, 1987.

_____. *Narrative Truth and Historical Truth.* New York: W. W. Norton, 1982.

Winkler, Karen J. "Scholars Prescribe Freud's 'Talking Cure' for Problems." *Chronicle of Higher Education,* 22, October 1986: 4–6.

Winnicott, D.W. *Playing and Reality.* London: Tavistock, 1971.

Zipes, Jack. *The Trials and Tribulations of Little Red Riding Hood.* So. Hadley, MA: Bergin and Garvey Publishers, 1983.

CHAPTER 1

Regression and the Fragmentation of the Self in *James and the Giant Peach*

Mark I. West

Roald Dahl's fantasies for children have long been popular with young readers, but they have not always been given a warm reception by critics. Instead of winning awards, his fantasies have tended to arouse controversy. His books have been accused of being vulgar, excessively violent, and disrespectful toward adults. Recently, however, Dahl's critical standing has improved. During the 1983 World Fantasy Convention, Dahl was given the organization's annual Life Achievement Award. *BFG, The Witches,* and *Matilda* have received a number of highly favorable reviews in such mainstream periodicals as *Horn Book* and the *New York Times Book Review.*[1]

Dahl's fantasies have even begun to attract scholarly attention. In a recent article published in *Signal,* Charles Sarland suggests that many of the criticisms of Dahl's fantasies are based on superficial readings. Dahl's writing, he argues, "is a good deal more complex than many commentators would have had us believe." Although Sarland focuses his article on *The Twits,* his argument can also be applied to Dahl's first children's book, *James and the Giant Peach.* A psychoanalytic interpretation of this book indicates that it is considerably more than an exciting, transatlantic adventure story.

Since its original publication in 1961, *James and the Giant Peach* has never been out of print.[2] Part of its long-standing appeal is undoubtedly its ingenious and fast-moving plot. However, one need not scratch very far beneath the surface of the story to discover another reason for its popularity among children. In an unobtrusive way, Dahl's tale deals with a common theme of children's fantasies: the urge to regress psychologically. Dahl recognizes this urge and provides children with a framework to work through their own fantasies about regression.

As Anna Freud, Melanie Klein, and others have pointed out, children often engage in regressive fantasies when faced with ego threatening problems and anxieties. Such is clearly the case with the hero of *James and the Giant Peach*. James is a seven-year-old orphan who lives with two cruel aunts. He feels abused, unwanted, unloved, and he strongly dislikes his aunts. On the day that his adventure begins, he begs his aunts to permit him to stop working and to take him to the seaside. They, of course, refuse, threaten to beat him, and call him a "disgusting little worm" (7). James flees from his aunts and begins crying over his unfortunate lot in life. Recognizing that a real-life James would likely begin fantasizing at this point, Dahl chooses this scene to interject the first fantasy element into the story.

While James is crying, he meets a peculiar but fatherly old man who gives James a bag full of "thousands of little green things" that were "slowly stirring about and moving over each other as though they were alive" (9). When James asks what these spermlike things are, he is told that they are magic crocodile tongues. James accidentally spills the bag near a scrawny peach tree, and the crocodile tongues quickly wriggle their way into the earth. Soon after this symbolic portrayal of fertilization, the tree sprouts a magical peach.

The peach grows to enormous proportions. While this miraculous phenomenon amazes the aunts, they are oblivious to the peach's beauty. They are primarily interested in exploiting the peach in order to make "a pile of money" (20). The aunts begin selling tickets to the curious for the privilege of seeing the awesome fruit. After their first day of business, the aunts send James out into the night to pick up the litter left by the onlookers. James is hungry, lonely, and afraid of the night. He longs to run away to someplace safe and warm. He longs to escape his problems and start over again. He unconsciously longs, Dahl suggests, to return to the womb.

Dahl fulfills James' wish in a most creative way. Toward the bottom of the peach, James discovers a tunnel leading toward the fruit's center, and he promptly enters it. What follows is a scene that closely resembles a reversal of the birthing process:

> The tunnel was damp and murky, and all around him was the curi-
> ous bittersweet smell of fresh peach. The floor was soggy under his
> knees, the walls were wet and sticky, and peach juice was dripping
> from the ceiling. James opened his mouth and caught some of it on
> his tongue. It tasted delicious. He was crawling uphill now, as
> though the tunnel were leading straight toward the very center of
> the gigantic fruit [25].

Upon reaching the peach stone, James finds a door which he uses to enter the stone. Once inside he encounters a menagerie of gigantic insects. They warmly welcome James, and one of them says to him, "You are one of us now" (28). Although there are seven insects, only four—the Ladybug, the Old-Green-Grasshopper, the Centipede, and the Earthworm—are central characters in the story. When viewed from a psychological perspective, these four bugs can be seen as separate aspects of James's own psychological makeup.

The fragmentation of the personality is actually a fairly common phenomenon during periods of regression. In the 1940s, Melanie Klein used the word "splitting" to describe this process. Although there is some disagreement over the definition of splitting, the word has entered the lexicon of psychologists and psychiatrists. As it is generally used, splitting occurs when an individual begins to regard various aspects of his or her personality as separate entities rather than as features of a unified whole. These divisions are usually products of introjection or projection. When introjection comes into play, the individual draws upon memories of another person, usually a parent, to create an internalized representation of that person (also known as an introject). When projection comes into play, the individual attempts to externalize certain parts of his or her personality by projecting these qualities onto another being.[3] Dahl makes use of both of these mechanisms in *James and the Giant Peach*.

The Ladybug and the Old-Green-Grasshopper both appear to be introjects. Dahl portrays them as kindly parents. They look after James, praise him when he does well, and share their knowledge with him. Unlike the cruel aunts, they provide James with the love that he so desperately needs. Although James' original parents died when he was four, Dahl suggests that they live on, at least in James' mind, in the form of these two insects.

The Centipede and the Earthworm are projections of James' id and can be seen as competing phallic symbols. The Centipede proudly proclaims himself to be a pest. He boasts, makes trouble, sings risqué songs, and indulges in wild dances. He corresponds, in some ways, to Freud's notion of Eros. The Earthworm, in contrast, is an impotent figure. He is powerless, whining, and defeated, and he constantly criticizes the Centipede. The Earthworm resembles Freud's conception of Thanatos or the self-destructive instinct. Important tensions within James' psyche are played out through the antics of these adversaries.

Soon after entering the peach, James and the Centipede form a close but lopsided relationship. The Centipede immediately begins ordering James about, and James attempts to obey the Centipede's every command. For example, before James and the insects retire for the night, the Centipede insists that James remove the Centipede's twenty-one pairs of boots. James, in other words, allows himself to be controlled by his id. In the morning, the Centipede continues to play a dominant role. He climbs out of the peach and chews through the stem that anchors the giant peach to the tree. Since the peach is resting on a steep slope, it starts rolling downhill.

The first objects that the peach rolls over are the cruel aunts, leaving them "as flat and thin and lifeless as a couple of paper dolls cut out of a picture book" (40). The death of the aunts plays a pivotal role in the story, for it represents the surfacing of James' murderous feelings toward his caretakers. As soon as these feelings are unleashed, James' safe peach stone turns into a chaotic pit. While the peach tumbles down the hill, James and his companions are violently tossed about. Frightened by the turn of events, James switches his allegiance from the Centipede to the Earthworm. When the peach finally comes to rest in the Atlantic Ocean, James and the Earthworm are wrapped around each other. Through these scenes, Dahl implies that James fears his own aggressive impulses and seeks to deny these impulses by embracing the impotent Earthworm. Dahl, however, does not allow James to remain in this defeated position.

Once the peach is floating peacefully in the ocean, James begins to rebuild his personality. He breaks his bond with the Earthworm and ventures out of the peach stone. Although he remains on top of the peach, he no longer seems to need the security of the womb. James is immediately confronted with numerous problems, but he bravely and cleverly solves each one. When the insects fear that they will starve, he explains that they can eat the peach. When sharks begin attacking the peach, James manages to turn the peach into an airship by tying hundreds of seagulls to the stem of the peach. Each time he solves a problem, the Ladybug and the Old-Green-Grasshopper congratulate him. Their praise helps James gain a sense of self-respect that he never had while he was living with the aunts.

As James begins to take control of his life, his relationship with the Centipede starts to change. Rather than feeling threatened by the Centipede, James grows to enjoy the Centipede's jokes and sardonic songs.

Dahl underscores this change in a dramatic scene that follows one of the Centipede's wild singing sprees. The Centipede gets so carried away with his singing and dancing that he falls off the peach and lands in the ocean far below. Much to the Earthworm's disappointment, James immediately sets out to rescue the Centipede. After attaching himself to a strand of string, James dives into the ocean and swims around until he finds the floundering Centipede. The other insects then hoist the two of them back up to the peach. Through this symbolic acceptance of his id, James indicates that he can cope with his inner tensions. He has learned that he need not renounce his id in order to control it.

Night falls soon after the rescue of the Centipede, and James and his companions have several more adventures before the sun reappears. Throughout these adventures, James demonstrates that he is able to deal with a variety of problems. By the morning, he is ready to re-enter society. He is no longer the miserable, guilt-ridden, withdrawn character that he was in the beginning of the book. He has become, instead, a cheerful and capable boy who desires the company of other children.

The book reaches its climax with James' rebirth, an event that takes place over New York City. James is drifting over the city when an airplane flies through the strings that attach the peach to the seagulls. Like a newborn infant who has been detached from the umbilical cord, James makes a sudden entrance into society. The peach plunges to earth, and James fears he will die when it hits the ground. His life is spared, though, because the peach falls on the Empire State Building and becomes impaled on the building's spire. Thus, James owes his life to a symbolic representation of sexual intercourse, just as a newborn infant's life stems from the sexual union of his or her parents.

After his adventure, James successfully recovers from his period of regression. Although he occasionally visits with the Ladybug, the Old-Green-Grasshopper, and the Centipede, he generally succeeds in reintegrating his fragmented personality. He allows the children of New York City to eat the peach, but he does not give away the peach stone. He has it moved to Central Park where he converts it into a snug house. Although James views the stone as his permanent home, he frequently ventures out of it and willingly allows other children to enter it. Thus, he uses the stone, not as a place to withdraw from society, but as a foundation upon which to build a social life. The peach stone seems to provide him with the type of security often associated with maternal love. Because he has this security, he is able to make friends and sustain his self-confidence. In short, he learns how to cope with the demands of both his internal world and the external environment.

Dahl is certainly not alone in suggesting that regression can be a positive experience. Ernst Kris and Heinz Hartmann, two prominent psychological theorists, argue that the suspension of ego control can sometimes help people deal with anxieties, and Anna Freud maintains that temporary ego regressions are a normal aspect of child development. Of course, no psychologist or psychiatrist would suggest that regression is always positive. In an attempt to distinguish healthy regression from pathological forms of regression, Michael J. Miller writes that "regression in the service of the ego ... has a definite beginning and end, is completely reversible, and is a function of successful adaptation to stress or change." James' regression meets all of these criteria, and this may explain why many children find the story so satisfying.

Notes

1. Review of *BFG*, in *Horn Book* 59, (1983): 165; and Erica Jong, "The Boy Who Became a Mouse," review of *The Witches*, in the *New York Times Book Review*, 13 November 1983: 45; Review of *Matilda*, in *The New York Times Book Review*, 15 January 1989: 31.

2. Published by Alfred A. Knopf. Page citations in the text refer to this edition.

3. For more information about splitting, see Melanie Klein, *Contributions to Psychoanalysis, 1921–1945*. London: Hogarth Press, 1948; Paul W. Pruyser, "What splits in splitting? A scrutiny of the concept of splitting in psychoanalysis and psychiatry," *Bulletin of the Menninger Clinic* 39, (1975): 1–46; and Otto Kernberg, "Structural derivations of object relationships," *International Journal of Psychoanalysis* 47, (1966): 236–253.

Works Cited

Dahl, Roald. *James and the Giant Peach*. New York: Knopf, 1961.

Freud, Anna. "Regression as a Principle in Mental Development." *Bulletin of the Menninger Clinic* 27 (1963): 126–139.

Hartmann, Heinz. *Essays on Ego Psychology: Selected Problems in Psychoanalytic Theory*. New York: International Universities Press, 1964.

Kris, Ernst. *Psychoanalytic Explorations in Art*. New York: Schocken Books, 1964.

Miller, Michael J. "The Rorschach: Psychoanalytic Theoretical Implications." *Directions in Psychiatry* 4.5 (1984): 1–7.

Sarland, Charles. "*The Secret Seven* vs. *The Twits*: Cultural Clash or Cozy Combination?" *Signal* 42 (1983): 155–171.

CHAPTER 2

The Mysterious and the Uncanny in *Nancy Drew* and *Harriet the Spy*

Lucy Rollin

It may seem odd to compare Louise Fitzhugh's ground-breaking 1964 children's novel *Harriet the Spy* with the series of Nancy Drew mysteries pouring from the Stratemeyer Syndicate since 1930, even though their appeal is rooted in the same phenomenon: mystery. Nancy solves mysteries of stolen jewels and missing wills; Harriet solves mysteries of human behavior. One is a modern classic of realism, the other is light entertainment. One is highly individual, the other bland and predictable in style. However, from a psychoanalytic point of view, their treatment of mystery offers a clue to the lasting appeal of both. Nancy and Harriet both seek the solution to the transcendent mystery of human behavior, but Nancy's discoveries offer an illusory satisfaction which keeps us longing for more. Harriet's discoveries are less concrete, but ultimately more human. Nancy's solutions keep us reading more books; Harriet's keep us looking at ourselves and others with sympathy.

When Nancy Drew was created in 1930, she represented a powerfully appealing fantasy for teen and pre-teen girls: an attractive, well-mannered, intelligent girl from a comfortable home, whose independence (symbolized by her expert driving in that little blue roadster) gave her dignified access to the adult world. For Anne Scott MacLeod, Nancy "is the very embodiment of every girl's deepest yearning ... an image that combines the fundamental impulse of feminism with utter conventionality" (47).

The success of the books was immediate and lasting. Fitzhugh's Harriet, on the other hand, would hardly be anyone's fantasy. Although she represents the so-called New Realism of 1960s children's literature, she differs considerably from the frequently noble, independent, mature child characters in that genre (Vera and Bill Cleaver's protagonists, for example) because she is clumsy, unattractive, noisy, rude, and clearly neurotic. She is also funny and achingly familiar to most children, and to any adults who can get past their discomfort at the popularity of such a character and remember what being a child was really like.

The two characters share one obsession: both are compulsive snoops. Nancy can't wait to get away from her friends at times so she can sleuth; she accepts boyfriend Ned's attentions only when they are convenient, preferring skulking to dancing any time. Bobbie Ann Mason comments that "the entrance to her emotions and physical desires are closed up tight" (65), a characteristic established in the first novel *The Secret of the Old Clock*, when she manipulates her friends into helping her without their knowledge and worries about the case so much that her father orders her to go window shopping to get her mind off it. Much of her inner dialogue consists of variations on "I'm not going to give up; I'm sure I'll find a clue today!" Harriet also seems incapable of accepting her schoolmates as friends, preferring her notebook and spy route to their company. Like Nancy, she hides in alleyways, listens at doorways, and peeps through windows.

Spying is not a particularly unusual activity for children, though it may take many forms. Most listen at their parents' doors from time to time, or eavesdrop on adult phone conversations; it is a common way to learn about adult life, since adults hide so much from children. With Harriet and Nancy, however, spying has come to dominate their lives—a neurotic response which Freud explored in one of his most intriguing essays, "The Uncanny" (1919). In his examination of that particular combination of fascination and dread, which he called *unheimlich* and which is usually translated as a sense of the uncanny, he turned to a tale of a child's spying and its tragic consequences: E.T.A. Hoffmann's famous tale of mystery, *The Sandman*, first published in 1816. For him, the tale held a "quite unparalleled atmosphere of uncanniness" because of its treatment of the folklore figure of the Sandman and its motif of eyes. In the story, the boy Nathanael develops an obsessive fear of the Sandman, whom he believes not only casts sand in children's eyes to make them sleepy but steals the eyes of naughty children and feeds them to owls with hooked beaks, a story told to him by his nurse.

Nathanael becomes convinced that the old lawyer Coppelius (the name comes from the Italian for "eye-socket"), who visits his father, is indeed the Sandman. He hides in his father's study when Coppelius visits, witnessing a strange alchemical experiment, and when he is discovered, Coppelius almost blinds him with hot coals. This scene may be fantasy, may be real; his father dies mysteriously soon afterward.

Nathanael's obsession with eyes—he everywhere encounters spying, spyglasses, opticians, eyeglasses, and windows—continues into adulthood and ends in madness as he throws himself from a balcony at the apparition of Coppelius, screaming the words of the mysterious old lawyer—"Ah, nice-a eyes, nice-a eyes!" (167). Hoffmann's horrific expansion of a bit of folklore (now mostly hidden from popular eyes by its transformation into the cheerful ballet *Coppelia*) fascinated Freud particularly because it leaves the mystery unsolved. It also led him to speculate that the fear of blinding was related to the infantile fear of sexual knowledge and the punishment thereof—specifically castration.

As we might expect in books about spying, eyes are a central motif in the Nancy Drew mysteries and in *Harriet the Spy*. Nancy's villains generally have dark and shifty eyes, or dark and penetrating eyes. Nancy's own eyes tell her unfailingly when someone is dishonest, dangerous, or innocent. Harriet, too, is always watching others, but the motif becomes particularly powerful when her schoolmates find her notebook and others begin watching her: "She looked at all their eyes and suddenly Harriet M. Welsch was afraid. They just looked and looked and their eyes were the meanest eyes she had ever seen" (181). The next day at school she writes, "They are out to get me. The whole room is filled with mean eyes."

When Harriet spies on her friends as they build their spy-catcher clubhouse, a cat with one eye stares at her. When she slinks away, realizing they had formed the club to exclude her, "there were seven cats sitting looking at her. One of them had no eyes at all" (214). Harriet's own spying glasses have no lenses—another poignant detail suggesting her self-delusion and frustration—her blindness. Ultimately, unlike Nancy's, Harriet's eyes are turned inward, on her own pain.

On the surface, these novels seem hardly to suggest the castration complex that Freud found in Hoffmann's "The Sandman." But Freud sought beyond this single connection, toward other evidence of infantile fears and speculations. Ultimately, what he found was a subtle but powerful connection with the whole notion of *home*. The German word for the uncanny is *unheimlich*, that which is unfamiliar, strange, creepy; but its root is the German for home: *Heim*. To Freud's surprise, that which is comfortable and familiar has the same linguistic origin as that which is frightening and strange.

Certainly, for children, this oxymoron describes sex, and Bobbie Ann Mason believes that in the Nancy Drew tales, mysteries "are a substitute for sex, since sex is the greatest mystery of all for adolescents" (63). But I see *Harriet* as going a step further, as a kind of "metamystery," in which what is hidden is not only sex, but that for which sex is only part of the puzzle: the complex secret of home.

Nancy's sleuthing usually takes her into people's homes: elegant or crumbling mansions, tidy or decrepit farmhouses, summer houses, cellars, drawing rooms, back gardens. Even when she visits camps or inns, their atmosphere is homelike, cozy and comforting. To quote Mason again, "adventure is the superstructure, domesticity the bedrock" of the Nancy Drew mysteries (with no hint that these might contradict each other) (60). Within the coziness are people in the grip of strong feelings of anger, betrayal, and fear, but Nancy does not seem especially interested in those feelings. Keeping her own feelings (in Mason's phrase) "closed up tight," Nancy seeks only tangible objects in these domestic settings: wills, jewels, money, letters, notebooks. When these are restored, the mystery is solved and Nancy goes on to the next puzzle without a backward glance.

Harriet takes comfort in objects—her books, spy tools, tomato sandwiches, and especially her notebook—but she is not seeking them. Harriet spies because, as she says, she wants to know "everything in the world, everything, everything" indiscriminately. But when she asks direct questions, they always focus on one thing: "What does it feel like?" How does it feel to meet the person you're going to marry? How does it feel to be asked to get married? How does she feel when she misses her nurse, Ole Golly? Like Nancy, she spies on domestic scenes of high emotion, but she seems especially interested in emotions between parents and children, unconsciously choosing—as Hamida Bosmajian says in her *Touchstones* essay about the novel—the objects of her scrutiny (77). Unlike Nancy, she seeks not objects but the emotions themselves. On the last spying trip before she is caught in Mrs. Plumber's dumbwaiter and her friends find her notebook, Harriet observes climactic moments in the lives of her subjects. She sees the Robinsons with their new sculpture: an enormous wooden baby—"a fat, petulant, rather unattractive baby," its fat hands holding, "surprisingly, a tiny mother" (157). "Gazing at it in speechless joy," the Robinsons are arranging it so it will "dominate" the room. As she observes this, her own emotions are repressed. She writes none of her usually direct comments about this in her notebook; she only writes about missing Ole Golly—an entry which suggests how disturbing this image is to her.

Her next stop is the Dei Santis house, where their family argument about Fabio reaches its climactic moment with a car accident, Mrs. Dei Santis' hysterical swoon, and the revelation that Fabio has a job. Harriet, still keeping her own emotions under wraps, rejects their noisy happiness, but does comment directly: "My, my, better than a movie. It's such a happy ending I don't believe it for one minute" (163).

The chapter ends with her visit to the unhappy Harrison Withers missing his substitute children, his cats. This time she acknowledges his emotion, and hers: "She looked a long time. Then ... she wrote in her book: I will never forget that face as long as I live.... Do people look like that when they have *lost*?" (164). All of this leaves her "grumpy." That very night Harriet pretends to be an onion, probing the layers of feeling she has witnessed, and finally wondering at her own vague response: "I just feel funny all over" (171).

Spying on other people's lives usually leads her to question her own, and the questions often have to do with parents and children. She wonders if Pinky Whitehead's mother hates him, and whether the Robinsons might kill their baby if it weren't perfect. These musings culminate in her entry about Ole Golly and Mr. Waldenstein:

> Life is a great mystery.... I wonder if people act like this when they get married. How could she get married? Would Mr. Waldenstein come to live with us then? They could put their child in my room if they wanted to. I wouldn't mind. I don't think. Unless it was a very nosy child who tried to read my notebooks. Then I would smash it [97].

In her notebook Harriet has put it rather clumsily, but she has summed up life's great mystery: *home*—that container for powerful emotions, that Freudian knot of sex, parents, children, love, hate, generosity, jealousy, joy, and sorrow that represents the familiar and the mysterious at once.

When Freud approached the subject of the uncanny, he found a linguistic conundrum. He found that over time, *heimlich* and *unheimlich* had become interchangeable in usage, both referring to that which is familiar *and* hidden, known *and* secret, congenial *and* frightening: "this uncanny is in reality nothing new or foreign, but something familiar and old-established in the mind that has been estranged only by the process of repression" (47). The prefix *un-* was the token of that repression (51).

One could hardly wish for a better description of the complex phenomenon we call "home." Although home is familiar, it is full of secrets, especially for children. Harriet's spying and listening at home generally add to the mystery of her life—the mumbling of her parents behind the library door, the gaze of her parents at her antics, her mother's response to her questions about meeting her father for the first time. Even Ole Golly, the most familiar part of Harriet's life, doesn't help. She quotes Dostoyevsky to Harriet: "If you love everything, you will perceive the divine mystery in things." When Harriet asks what that means, Ole Golly stumbles over an explanation and finally subsides into "Well, that's about it..." (24)

At the climactic moment of the novel, she bursts into that famous bit of nonsense "The Walrus and the Carpenter," and in her letter to Harriet, part of the wisdom she dispenses is the most frustrating (and possibly meaningless) line in all English poetry: "Beauty is truth, and Truth, beauty; That is all ye know on earth and all ye need to know." She adds, "And don't you ever forget it" (275). When Ole Golly does tell the unvarnished truth, it is another conundrum: You have to lie to others but always tell yourself the truth. Bosmajian defends the novel as a touchstone of children's literature on just this point: its uncompromising honesty in telling children they have to compromise (82).

To every child, home is the great mystery—not only sex but a whole constellation of notions and feelings, onion-like in their layers, peeling away only to reveal another mystery: paternity, maternity, ambivalence, physical security, powerful emotions suppressed yet threatening, the preexisting place which yet seems so fragile. Nancy Drew's triumphant discoveries of wills, letters, or jewels provide only a momentary, illusory solution to the mystery.

In his pivotal essay "Beyond the Pleasure Principle," which he wrote the year following "The Uncanny," Freud described his young grandson's "*fort/da* game"—hiding his toys and joyfully discovering them, again and again, to control his anxiety over his mother's departures. This homely example was an instance of the infantile compulsion to repeat, which in young children is an effort at mastery, each repetition bringing only a measure of, rather than complete, success (599–611). This is one reason—to me a fundamental one—that Nancy Drew books and similar light detective fiction usually exist in series. The detective is like a child, continually repeating the search for what is hidden and finding no real satisfaction. Nancy is a "sleuth"—the word comes from the Middle English for an animal track—always tracking, always on the move, but finding only objects, not the realities behind them. Reading about her reminds us unconsciously of similar fruitless searches in our early childhood, which we can yet enjoy in this controlled way, just as Freud's grandson enjoyed his game. On the other hand, Harriet is a spy, watching in stillness, and eventually facing the real mystery of human relationships. We might read *Harriet* many times, but each time we will have the sense that we have come close, not to the solution itself, but at least to the nature of the "metamystery": ourselves in relation to others.

No wonder most of us like to indulge in what someone has called "the pleasures of the keyhole," in literature and in life. What we hope to find there, like Harriet, is "everything, everything."

Works Cited

Bosmajian, Hamida. "Louise Fitzhugh's *Harriet the Spy*: Sense and Nonsense." *Touchstones*, Vol. 1, 71–82. West Lafayette, IN: ChLA Publishers, 1985.

Fitzhugh, Louise. *Harriet the Spy*. New York: HarperTrophy, 1964.

Freud, Sigmund. "The Uncanny" (1919). In *Studies in Parapsychology*, ed. Philip Rieff. New York: Collier, 1963.

_____. "Beyond the Pleasure Principle" (1920). In *The Freud Reader*, ed. Peter Gay. 594–626. New York: W. W. Norton, 1989.

Hoffman, E.T.A. "The Sandman." In *Selected Writings of Hoffman*. Edited and translated by Kent and Knight. Vol. 1. Chicago: University of Chicago Press, 1969.

Keene, Carolyn. *The Secret of the Old Clock* (1930). Bedford, MA: Applewood Books, 1991.

Mason, Bobbie Ann. *The Girl Sleuth* (1975). Athens: University of Georgia Press, 1995.

MacLeod, Anne Scott. "Nancy Drew and Her Rivals: No Contest." *American Childhood: Essays on Children's Literature of the Nineteenth and Twentieth Centuries*. 30–48. Athens: University of Georgia Press, 1994.

CHAPTER 3

Uncanny Mickey Mouse and His Domestication

Lucy Rollin

It is now commonplace to say that Mickey Mouse represents "the child in all of us." By this we mean that he is playful, gentle, fun-loving, and innocent, that he represents a fresh view of the world, that Mickey's world is all sunshine, kindness, joy, peace, and equality. When Walt Disney created him, however, Mickey represented a different kind of child: sadistic, aggressive, mischievous—a remarkable icon of the primitive, id-driven child which civilization aims to repress. This transition, which took place in the late 1930s, is rooted, I believe, in Disney's intuitive ability to create an *uncanny* Mickey. In Freudian terms, the uncanny is the momentary emergence of our most irrational, primitive selves; it gives us a shiver of recognition and pleasure, but it also frightens us, often into the refuge of rationality. Once Mickey became frightening, he was eased into the safe, easily controlled world of popular children's books, where the uncanny is often repressed.

Although Freud's essay "The Uncanny" first appeared in 1919, he had evidently written much of it in earlier years and, probably realizing he was in dangerous territory for one who called himself a scientist, set it aside. All of Freud's work takes risks we cannot fully appreciate today, and this one gave his detractors more opportunity than usual for ridicule or contempt. But he persevered, and the result is one of his richest theoretical excursions into human thought.

31

As he saw it, our sense of the "uncanny"—prompted for example by unusual coincidences, the discovery of a double, the fear we feel when alone in silence and darkness—arises from the sense of something strange yet familiar, inexplicable yet fully present to the senses, a blurring of the distinction between the real and the imaginary. But in 1919 he had not yet imagined the peculiar art form of the cartoon film, in which the imaginary becomes more fully present to the senses than in anything literature or daily life could offer.

Disney's 1928 hit, *Steamboat Willie* with its manic mouse and its combination of fantasy, technology, and wild energy, framed in dream-like darkness as the strange yet familiar images flickered across the screen, would surely have been among the most uncanny of artifacts to merit Freud's attention. Nor is it likely that Disney had read Freud when he made *Plane Crazy* and *Steamboat Willie*, but the characteristics of his early cartoons resemble, to a remarkable degree, Freud's catalogue of ingredients for the uncanny.

Freud begins by agreeing with E. Jentsch's description of a successful uncanny effect in art: the creation of uncertainty whether a particular figure is a human being or something else—"an automaton"—but without focusing attention on this uncertainty (31). All the anthropomorphous figures in the early cartoons revel in this uncertainty without giving us time to think about their oddity, instead making our eyes race to keep up with their frantic fighting, dancing, or music-making. They seem to be animal, human, and machine at once, and at will.

In *Plane Crazy*, a 1928 silent film that actually predates *Steamboat Willie* but which was released later, the early, more rodent-like Mickey succeeds in making his hair look like Charles Lindbergh's; the "engine" in his plane is a dachshund with Mickey's head and face, which twists itself up like a spring and then unwinds, making the propeller of Mickey's plane spin. Caroline the Cow, chasing Mickey's departing plane with Mickey on her back, stretches her neck longer and longer until it snakes across the entire screen like a rubber tube. After a crash, Mickey snatches the entire tail from a turkey to replace the tail on his plane.

Such film characters have always been "automatons": products of technology and artifice. Yet we usually think of Mickey as both mouse and human. Even Disney called him "a pretty nice fellow," disingenuously keeping the uncanny effect alive.

Doubling, among the most uncanny of phenomena in life as well as in literature, also appears early in Mickey cartoons. Mickey has always had a double: Minnie. They look exactly alike except for a few minor details of clothing and eyelashes; moreover, Minnie's functions correspond to those of Rank's *Doppelgänger*, which Freud recaps (40).[1] From its origins as a kind of comforting insurance against death, it grew into a fearsome reminder of death, and then into a separate entity which observes the ego and which we call a conscience. This evolutionary pattern reflects the development of the infant from primary narcissism, with its pride and sense of immortality, to the older child's awareness of its fragility and its ability to observe itself critically.

Minnie narcissistically admires Mickey's heroism, absolutely certain that he can do anything, even fly a homemade plane with a dachshund as an engine. She also represents his vulnerable side with her squealing fear of death and destruction every time they get into trouble. And she fulfills the role of his conscience by sometimes making him behave—as when she socks him for stealing a kiss in the airplane. Like the mysterious double in many works of fiction, she turns up in his adventures all over the world. Mickey and Minnie flirt, express affection, and often live together in what is apparently a sexless marriage, but their union is nonetheless essential.

It is as if, from the very beginning, one mouse alone would not do; in an intuitive return to the primitive notion of the double, Disney gave his creation a double which assured his completeness and his immortality, allowing him to revel in physical risk and violence, and then took the next evolutionary step by making Minnie his conscience.

Another primitive psychological mechanism which characterizes the uncanny and which for Freud remains harbored in our unconscious is what he (and the late 19th century anthropologist Edward Tylor) calls *animism*: the belief that all things, animate and inanimate, contain spirits just as humans do. The technique of animation, Disney's hallmark, is the visual, mechanical enactment of this ancient idea and is one of the fundamental reasons for Disney's phenomenal appeal across cultures. Dancing severed body parts and living skeletons, two ingredients in worldwide folklore, are staples from the early Disney cartoons and reflect the animistic mind which sees life in everything.

As we observe the plasticity of Mickey's body, his ability—and that of all cartoon characters—to survive plane crashes and falls, or the dancing skeletons he encounters in "The Haunted House," we are linked once again with this long-repressed notion which gives unconscious pleasure because it unites all creation and affirms the existence of the soul. Consciously we escape death with Mickey when he escapes death over and over in these early cartoons; unconsciously we triumph over death even more when we see him as part of a larger cartoon world in which all things are animate—and more than animate: full of extraordinary energy which never stops to question its mystery or source. None of our response to this and other elements of the uncanny is rational but it is therefore all the more powerful, rooted as it is in infantile fantasies and primitive modes of thought long repressed.

The famous Russian filmmaker Sergei Eisenstein was a great admirer of the early Mickey Mouse. Like other truly great artists, Eisenstein said in 1941, Disney "creates on the conceptual level of man not yet shackled by logic, reason, or experience" (2). Eisenstein traces the rubbery arms and legs of the pre-color Mickey through their evolution as a visual motif— their appearance in Chinese art, the stretching neck of Tenniel's Alice in Wonderland—and speculates that their appeal lies in the visual suggestion of "all possible diversity of form"; he stops short of agreeing with Freud that this quality triggers an unconscious memory, but he does link it with the omnipotence and narcissism of our pre-civilized selves (10–21).

Around the same time, psychoanalyst Fritz Moellenhoff offered an equally admiring psychoanalytic assessment of Mickey's cartoon films which focused on Disney's intuitive representation of "a child's world of wishes and fantasies" (111). In addition to their elements of sadism and asexuality, he cited the films' disregard of physical law, their lack of causality, their "eternal gaiety and unfounded optimism." The cartoon Mickey allows us to witness the ego allied with the id, without superego interference—a state of affairs usually unavailable to anyone except infants and sociopaths. "Who would not," Moellenhoff asked, "enjoy this situation?" (118)

He was begging the question. Although Eisenstein and Moellenhoff were enjoying it, many ordinary movie-goers were not. By 1939, Mickey's character had begun to change partly because audiences were increasingly offended when he got violent. David Bain and Bruce Harris say that Disney received "an avalanche of letters every time Mickey kicked someone in the pants" (24)—i.e. when moviegoers saw that uncontrolled id on the big screen. Bain and Harris also comment that Mickey's popularity was declining at the same time that the demand for animated short films was diminishing, that Disney's high standard of animation was increasingly expensive to produce and make profitable, and that animators began to have trouble coming up with "plots and believable settings for a four-foot mouse … Mickey was too out of proportion with his environment" (24–27), although neither animators nor audiences seemed to have trouble with Mickey's proportions in the early films.

Disney himself was, and apparently wanted to be, increasingly identified with Mickey; since his kindly "Uncle Walt" image hardly fit the manic early mouse, the sadism and frantic energy were transferred to Donald Duck, while Mickey abandoned his short pants for suits, ties, and snap-brim hats, moved to the suburbs, and became father to his nephews (Bain and Harris 24). Mickey's withdrawal from his own films and his increasing role (frequently alongside Walt—another instance of doubling?) as host/patriarch/entrepreneur, was probably rooted in all these causes—an instance of what Freud called over-determination. But from a psychoanalytic point of view, Mickey's uncanny qualities—especially his primary narcissism and manic actions—while on the one hand making him enormously appealing, were also becoming too threatening to his creators and his audience.[2]

Disney evidently planned to reawaken audience interest in Mickey by starring him in *The Sorcerer's Apprentice*, the story of a young magician's apprentice who misuses the magician's powers. Mickey's smallness and increasingly infantile appearance worked perfectly against the tall magician and the multiplying brooms and the overwhelming water pouring from the buckets. But Disney also became fascinated with the idea of a concert film, featuring various short cartoons set to classical music, of which the Mickey film would be only one. His collaboration with conductor Leopold Stokowski and his heavy investment in sophisticated sound equipment for what became *Fantasia* caused it to become much more than a vehicle for Mickey. When it was released in 1940 (much trimmed from Disney's original version of it), audiences who loved the innocent Mickey left the theater puzzled and irritated because it wasn't a fairy tale (Jackson 33).

A more pervasive part of Disney's response to the threat the "old" Mickey posed was to change his appearance. Mickey had already become more childlike, as had most of the animals in Disney's cartoon features. Disney seemed to have an uncanny ability to tap into the human "cute response," as biologists have called it: the desire to nurture and protect anything that has babylike qualities—large head and eyes, round tummy, small rounded arms and legs, etc.[3] Now there were efforts to make him more "human." In the early 1940s the studio was ordered to remove Mickey's tail "for economic reasons" and artists began experimenting with ears drawn in perspective, giving him a three dimensional appearance (Holliss and Sibley 43–44). The "new" Mickey never gained the popularity of the old on the screen, even with the animators themselves, but when he began to appear in children's books, he was more successful.

Mice have long been appealing characters in children's fantasies; their size, cleverness, quickness, and vulnerability make them excellent analogues of childhood. Beatrix Potter tapped into their destructive side in 1905 with her *Tale of Two Bad Mice*. But Mickey's domestication represents a broad movement which has been repeated many times in children's books, especially those that aim for the popular market. The great uncanny classics of children's literature—*The Adventures of Alice in Wonderland, Pinocchio, The Wind in the Willows*—in their original forms have become the province of adulthood, some say, too "sophisticated" or "difficult" for today's children. A more fundamental problem is their direct links to our uncivilized selves— to the uncanny that represents true childhood.

The shift is even more visible when folklore enters print. The old tales of *Rapunzel* and *Little Red Riding Hood* lose their violence and magic when they are tamed into ordinary—or even worse, politically correct— yarns. The uncanny, said Freud, "arouses dread and creeping horror"; it is a "class of the terrifying"(19–20). Although he exempted fairy tales from his definition of the uncanny in literature because they announced right away their faerie-world settings, and hence did not excite the same fears as literature set in the "real" world, the constant revision and censorship of the tales suggest that unconsciously we fear their primitive origins for the same reason that we fear other uncanny phenomena: they remind us of something we want to forget.

The Mickey of the early 1930s was, in this sense, also terrifying, perhaps even more frightening because he was shared by adults and children, and most rational, civilized adults do not want to share (at least consciously) their primitive natures with their children. Primitive fantasies in children's books which aim for a wide market have for centuries been sacrificed to didacticism and rationality, at least in the publishing world where adults reign supreme; the Disney studio in the late 1930s was only the richest and most famous participant in the process.[4]

Books based on Mickey films were successfully marketed for children throughout the 30s, and while some lip service was paid to a sentimental view of children and what their books should say, their material was usually as manic and violent as the cartoons themselves. Some were published in the form of "Big Little Books," fat books printed on cheap paper, which reproduced the feel of the cartoons as the reader rapidly turned the pages. In many of these Mickey talks like a street tough: "And to think I was kickin' about MY hard luck! Gee! If I had a lot o'money, it'd sure be fun t' sneak in there with a whole bag full o' food and stuff for 'em!" (*Movie Stories* 12). But some make more of an effort to be childlike, at least in the conventional sense. One cartoon, "The Birthday Party," when written as a 1931 book for children, adopted a strained combination of prose and poetry, its dialogue sounding banal when no longer accompanied by music and visual action: "Oh hello Mickey." "Hello Minnie!" "How are you, Mickey?" "Oh I'm fine, Minnie, and how are you?"

The pictures in this book are just as primitive as those in the cartoon, however. When Mickey blows out his candles, all the frosting blows right into the face of the cook, a huge pig; later during the dancing the pig's clothes split and his trousers come off as the partygoers "wiggled and jiggled and clapped and slapped." Mickey attacks a xylophone, which comes to life and dances; Mickey rides it like a horse and lands on his chin, then "he hit the pedestal holding the goldfish bowl. And the bowl came CRASH down over Mickey's head and stayed there. In fact, it stuck so tightly on Mickey's shoulders that the water all stayed in, and everybody cheered while the fish swam around and around his face and tickled him on the nose."

The unusual mix of this violent, irrational action with conventional notions of a children's book is especially noticeable in the next, and last, lines:

> Gee, wouldn't it be glorious
> If every day could be
> A birthday just like Mickey's was
> For folks like you and me?
>
> [reprinted in Bain and Harris 169]

The Disney folks were attempting to blend their uncanny, genuinely infantile, primitive, sadistic cartoons with a vague, popular, sentimental notion of what should be in a children's book, and the result was most peculiar.

Stories not taken from cartoons, but written specifically for the Mouse, also appeared early though much less frequently. In 1930, eleven-year-old Bobette Bibo, daughter of a member of the publishing firm Bibo and Lang, contributed "The Story of Mickey Mouse" to a Mickey book. Her tale has the Mouse thrown out of "mouse fairyland" for his misbehavior, landing in Hollywood, and being discovered by Mr. Disney. At first her Mickey is as manic and untamed as the early cartoon mouse; then he becomes a big star (by this time Minnie has magically appeared on the scene as "his sweetheart") and becomes more civilized, driving a limo and sleeping peacefully at the foot of Disney's bed (Bain and Harris 160–164).

By 1939, as Mickey's screen popularity waned, the Disney studio began commissioning more children's books with original stories written by adults. One of these, published in 1939 by the D. C. Heath Company and

written by Robin Palmer, offers a remarkable—one may say uncanny—
image of the more civilized Mouse *in statu nascendi. Mickey Never Fails* is
an early "chapter book," written probably for a reader aged 5–8 and containing only a few illustrations in its hundred-plus pages. In it Mickey has
completely shed his animal identity but hovers between child and adult in
a string of events as casually linked as dreams. He is truly, to use Sergei
Eisenstein's admiring word, *protoplasmic* (69), but what is being born is a
Mickey who, instead of linking us directly with our primitive psychic begin-
nings as the uncanny always does, has begun to separate us from them.

In the story, Mickey takes possession of a new house and invites Minnie, her twin nephews Monty and Morty, and her Aunt Matilda to live
with him. As did the early Mickey, this one manages to solve every problem, through either luck or cleverness. But Mickey's dual identities as child
and as adult seem dissonant in this text. As he watches the workmen build
his house (which he had come across accidentally while wandering the
woods), "Sometimes he helped them, and sometimes he played with the
plaster and cement. He even tasted things." On another page, he explains
that he wants the house because it has an oil burner to heat it, "and hot
water too. I'll be able to take a hot bath whenever I please.... Running
water is useful." Strange noises begin to plague the house. Minnie, squealing "Help! Help!" is convinced it is a bear, and Mickey brags that he can
fight a bear. When the growling continues, he nervously ventures down to
investigate, and discovers it was only the oil burner coming on. He returns
and earnestly, father-like, explains to the others, "It's a machine that burns
oil and heats the house. When the machine goes on, it makes a growling
noise, a loud one when it starts, and a softer one while it is running. Then
the house gets warm, so it turns itself off. And when the house gets cold,
it starts running and heats it up again" (69).

At one point, in their efforts to establish Mickey as part of the world
of children's literature, the author and editors insert a bizarre echo of the
self-conscious tone of *Winnie the Pooh*. Like Pooh indulging in one of his
"hums," Mickey makes up a little poem celebrating the hot water, and
when Minnie praises him for it, he demurs, "Of course, it isn't like Stevenson." Minnie protests, "Yes, of course it is. Stevenson couldn't touch it,"
and Mickey says, "Oh come, come, you don't know Stevenson"—but is "very
much pleased" (74–75).

Minnie expresses the desire for a crocodile as a pet. One day while
Mickey is wandering in the woods and feeling the pressure of his responsibilities toward the others—"I almost wish I didn't own a house," he
thinks—he sits down on a crocodile. He is frightened at first and hides on

a roof, but the crocodile seems tame. He invites it home and introduces it to the others, who are frightened at first: "'Bite?' cried Mickey. 'A friendly crocodile like this? Of course not. You shall ride him around the furnace room. He's quite a safe pet, really. Aren't you, Alfred?... I thought I should call him Alfred. It's such a nice, proper name'" (99).

No doubt Robin Palmer (a pseudonym perhaps?) and the editor of this text aimed to produce something childlike, which for them involved chiefly an innocent pleasure in physical play and a random plot. But they also seem to want an adult Mickey, an ambivalence which even the few illustrations reveal: one shows him sitting in a puddle looking distressed and distinctly childlike, another shows him laughing at the oil burner and looking quite grown-up. At any rate, gone are the truly infantile fears, wishes, and perceptions—the uncanny elements—of the early Mickey cartoon stories.

The early Mickey never explained anything, or even paused for reflection. This Mickey explains away the mysteries of weird noises in the cellar and fierce wild beasts in the forests, shining the bland light of rationality in their place. By the end of the story, Mickey is firmly in place as the patriarch of this extended family, where he remains today in countless Little Golden Books—and in the Magic Kingdom, a diminutive adult gate-keeper allowing only so much access to our primitive selves and no more, a symbol of the repression at which he once so joyfully thumbed his rodent nose.

As Bain and Harris have noted, this change in Mickey Mouse had a whole complex of causes. Disney's own personality, studio finances, audience response, the increasing popularity of other characters, animators' difficulties, and the advent of television all played a part. On a larger scale, perhaps the Depression-ridden 30s needed a figure on which to project its fantasies of violence and immortality as people daily faced great uncertainties about their personal futures, while the early 40s witnessed events more violent and horrifying than their fantasies could construct. Then movie-goers needed their rational adulthood to survive, and they needed to protect their children from the dreadful things they saw in the world. Their beloved Mickey became a symbol of their good sense and loving parenthood.

Kathy Jackson sees a patriotic motive for the change as well: "As Mickey became more and more of an American institution, he began to embody the attributes of the country he represented: he was brave, kind, trustworthy, hard-working, and loyal" (16). But he was no longer uncanny. For a short time, sharing our ancient humanity in the form of a funny mouse was pleasant, but when Mickey became too loved, too much a conscious image of ourselves, the primitivism became too threatening. The uncanny nature of the early Mickey gradually diffused into Disney's other characters, into the genial and silently waving host at the Magic Kingdom, and into the safety of words on a page—and something original and remarkable was lost.

But the old Mickey has sneaked in by the back door. The 1960s marked the appearance of the "New Realism" in children's books; Louise Fitzhugh's *Harriet the Spy* and Maurice Sendak's *Where the Wild Things Are* shocked some adults because of their frank depiction of children's rage and compulsiveness. One of these books, Sendak's *In the Night Kitchen*, deliberately recreates the 1930s mouse. Born like Mickey in 1928 and an ardent fan of the early Mickey, Sendak describes, in his introduction to the 1988 reprint of *Mickey Mouse Movie Stories*, how he screamed with delight and "with Pavlovian regularity" when he beheld Mickey's smile on the screens of the movie houses in his Brooklyn neighborhood during the Depression. He, too, bemoans Mickey's transformation into a conventional adult figure, and so in the 1960s he created his own Mickey, the hero of his best-selling and controversial 1972 picture book *In the Night Kitchen*. Sendak's Mickey falls naked from his bed, is baked in an oven in bread dough, encounters three somewhat sadistic bakers who all look exactly like Oliver Hardy, flies in a dough airplane (a direct reference to *Plane Crazy*), swims in milk, and enjoys a host of primitive physical dangers and sensations in a thumpingly rhythmic text and in pictures filled with the manic energy of the early Mickey Mouse cartoons.

The book ends with Sendak's Mickey triumphant, surrounded by radiating yellow beams, just as was Mickey Mouse in his trademark portrait. "This book," says Sendak, "encapsulated my passion for Mickey, movies, New York City, and the strange, dark, doomful Thirties that for me, were lit only by Mickey's bright beaming smile on the screen" (*Mickey Mouse Movie Stories* Introduction, unpaged).

Still, it is not pleasant for most adults to be reminded of what lies beneath our civilized exteriors, especially in a children's book. Their fear springs from repression and makes itself known often in censorship of one kind or another. Many parents were too uncomfortable with it to share the book with their children. Many librarians added magic-marker diapers to Sendak's full-frontally nude Mickey, just as Disney tamed his wild Mickey into long pants and bow ties. (Sendak once commented in an interview that he imagined children all over America holding their books up to the light to see under those diapers, since they probably already knew what was there.)

Try as we might, though, children will return to the primitivism of the uncanny all by themselves. They love all the old animistic ideas: doubles, severed body parts which dance, the blending of a human with an animal body, living skeletons. Perhaps, as Freud's American disciple G. Stanley Hall suggested, children carry in themselves the pre-history of the race (see deCordova 211–213).

Children's own folklore certainly offers evidence that they enjoy the primitive. In the 1940s and 50s, Iona and Peter Opie studied the folklore and language British and American children use in the schoolyard when adults are not interfering or prescribing. The second most popular figure to appear in the schoolyard taunts and games they heard was Mickey Mouse (the first was Charlie Chaplin), and in an interesting example of Freudian primary process, the children often created their jingles around the *mouse/house* rhyme:

> All around the house
> To look for Mickey Mouse,
> If you catch him by the tail
> Hang him on a rusty nail,
> Give him to the cook.
>
> Mickey Mouse, in his house,
> Taking off his trousers.
> Quick, Mum, smack his bum,
> And chase him round the houses.
>
> Mickey Mouse is dead,
> He died last night in bed.
> He cut his throat
> With a ten bob note,
> Mickey Mouse is dead.
>
> [Opie 111]

One of the most fascinating moments in Freud's essay "The Uncanny" is his unpacking of the German word for "uncanny": *unheimlich*. Through an exhaustive etymological analysis, he discovers that *heimlich*—originally meaning familiar, homelike—and *unheimlich* have evolved until they share the same meaning: "this uncanny is in reality nothing new or foreign, but something familiar and old-established in the mind that has been estranged by the process of repression" (47). Ironically, just about the same time that

Disney thought he had tidied up the 1930s Mickey into a symbol of conventional adulthood and repressed his uncanniness, children were, on the sly, keeping the old uncanny Mickey alive, at home—*heimlich*—and as *unheimlich* as ever.

Notes

1. From a Jungian perspective, she is also his *anima*, his soul-image which provides him with internal completeness and balance through her feminine essence; he is her *animus*. Charles Hampden-Turner comments that romantic love is "often an infatuation with one's own soul-image" (46), a description which certainly fits the narcissistic nature of their relationship.

2. The complete Mickey filmography which appears on the last page of Holliss and Sibley offers a visual map of his career: the majority of films were made in 1932, holding steady until 1937, 1938 and 1939, with a marked decrease thereafter. The last Mickey film was made in 1953, until he appeared again as the kindly Bob Cratchit in the 1983 Disney version of *A Christmas Carol*—a character perfectly embodying the mature Mickey: kind, gentle, self-effacing, a bit ineffectual but winning—light-years away from *Steamboat Willie*.

3. See James Serpell, who compares the "cute response" to the parasitic cuckoo, which is cared for tenderly by the songbirds whose nest it has invaded (62). He also cites Stephen Jay Gould's comments on Disney animators who design their products to elicit the response, to their financial advantage.

4. Richard deCordova attributes Disney's success in merchandising Mickey toys, which began early and reached enormous proportions in the mid and late 30s, to similar phenomena but with a different emphasis. Mickey's animality allied him with the primitive world, but he was also "aggressively modern," as were movie-going children (often to the despair of parents and reformers). But since toys are a conventional part of childhood, Mickey toys centered the Mouse in a more familiar tradition: "the merchandising worked more assuredly than the movies to push the image of the child back into traditional categories of childhood" (213). So did the image of the new Mickey in children's books.

Works Cited

Bain, David, and Bruce Harris. *Mickey Mouse: Fifty Happy Years*. New York: Harmony Books, 1977.

deCordova, Richard. "The Mickey in Macy's Window." In *Disney Discourse: Producing Magic Kingdom*. Ed. Eric Smoodin. 203–213. New York: Routledge, 1994.

Eisenstein, Sergei. *Eisenstein on Disney*. Ed. Jay Leyda, trans. Alan Upchurch. New York: Methuen, 1988.

Freud, Sigmund. "The Uncanny." In *Studies in Parapsychology*, ed. Philip Rieff. 19–60. New York: Collier Books, 1963.

Gould, Stephen Jay. "Mickey Mouse meets Konrad Lorenz." *Natural History*, May 30, 1979.

Hampden-Turner, Charles. *Maps of the Mind*. New York: Collier, 1982.

Holiss, Richard, and Brian Sibley. *Walt Disney's Mickey Mouse: His Life and Times.* New York: Harper and Row, 1986.

Jackson, Kathy Merlock. *Walt Disney: A Biobibliography.* Westport, CT: Greenwood Press, 1993.

Mickey Mouse Movie Stories (1934). Story and illustration by staff of Walt Disney Studio. Intro. by Maurice Sendak. New York: Harry N. Abrams, 1988.

Moellenhoff, Fritz. "Remarks on the Popularity of Mickey Mouse" (1940). Reprinted in *American Imago* 46 (Summer-Fall 1989): 105–119.

Opie, Iona and Peter. *The Lore and Language of Schoolchildren.* London: Oxford University Press, 1959.

Palmer, Robin. *Mickey Never Fails.* Boston: D. C. Heath, 1939. (In the deGrummond Collection, University of Southern Mississippi, Hattiesburg.)

Sendak, Maurice. *In the Night Kitchen.* New York: HarperCollins, 1970.

Serpell, James. *In the Company of Animals.* Cambridge: Cambridge University Press, 1986.

CHAPTER 4

Narcissism in
The Wind in the Willows

Mark I. West

Of the four major characters in *The Wind in the Willows*, Toad has always been the favorite of young readers. This was true even before the book existed as a completed manuscript. Toad, along with Mole, Rat, and Badger, first appeared in bedtime stories that Kenneth Grahame told to his son Alastair. The boy took a special interest in Toad and delighted in hearing about Toad's misadventures. When Alastair was separated from his father during the summer of 1907, he asked him to send more letters about Toad's activities. Alastair's governess preserved these letters, and Grahame later used them as the basis for *The Wind in the Willows* (Elspeth Grahame 1–22).

Toad's popularity among children is certainly understandable. He is an exuberant troublemaker, and children are usually drawn to such characters. As Nicholas Tucker has pointed out in "The Children's Falstaff," Toad "dared do and express many of the things they may have often felt like doing, and such children could both feel superior to Toad's obvious deficiencies and excesses and also revel in them at the same time" (163). Toad's self-centeredness is another quality with which children can easily identify. Narcissistic tendencies, Freud argues in his essay "On Narcissism," are basic characteristics of infants, and more recent psychological theorists have suggested that these tendencies remain strong throughout adolescence (Hamilton 118–19). Thus, it is not surprising that children can relate to Toad's boastfulness as well as his egocentric view of the world.

Since Toad exhibits many childish qualities, it is tempting to view him as a child. A number of people have, in fact, taken this position. Lois R. Kuznets, for example, argues that Toad can "be seen as representative of a child struggling to control his impulses and tailor his needs to the demands of society" (111). Others have suggested that Toad is simply a caricature of Alastair (Green 282). These interpretations certainly explain some of Toad's immature acts, such as throwing temper tantrums. Some critics, however, feel that it is an oversimplification to regard Toad as a child in an amphibian's skin.

Grahame's biographer, Peter Green, feels that Toad should be viewed as an adult with a "queer pathological streak" (284). A careful examination of the text tends to bear out Green's interpretation. However childishly Toad may behave, Grahame never suggests that he is not an adult. He portrays Toad as an affluent but irresponsible young man. Like most adults, Toad is fairly independent. He controls a large estate and makes major purchasing decisions. He thinks of himself as a gentleman and is generally regarded as such by his peers.

There are several other factors that indicate that Grahame wants Toad to be thought of as an adult. Although most of the characters in *The Wind in the Willows* are animals, Grahame clearly indicates that some are adults and some are children. The Otter's son, Little Portly, is definitely a child. The field mice who sing Christmas carols to Mole and Rat are portrayed as children. Nowhere in the book, however, is Toad equated with these young animals. For the most part, they are expected to look up to Toad, a point that Grahame underscores in the book's conclusion:

> Sometimes, in the course of long summer evenings, the friends would take a stroll together in the Wild Wood,… and it was pleasing to see how respectfully they were greeted by the inhabitants, and how the mother weasels would bring their young ones to the mouths of their holes and say, pointing, "Look, baby! There goes the great Mr. Toad!" [258]

Toad also has little in common with the children whom Grahame so lovingly describes in two of his earlier books, *The Golden Age* and *Dream Days*. These characters exude innocence and gentleness, qualities that Toad obviously lacks. As Green convincingly argues, Grahame is much more inclined to associate negative qualities with adults than he is with children (177). For this reason, Green feels that Toad is modeled, not after Alastair, but after some of the eccentric adults with whom Grahame was familiar. The two examples whom Green mentions are Horatio Bottomley, a flamboyant politician (242–43), and Oscar Wilde (284). If Toad is seen as an adult, however, it becomes more difficult to account for some of his peculiar actions. One possible way to explain much of Toad's behavior is to view him as a narcissist.

Although *The Wind in the Willows* was written well before the coining of the phrase "narcissistic personality disorder," Grahame's portrayal of Toad could almost be a case illustration of this particular psychological problem. In addition to his exhibiting the surface characteristics of a narcissist, Toad's thought processes and basic behavior patterns closely resemble this personality type.

In describing Toad's personality, Grahame anticipates some later theories on narcissism. Most psychological theorists who have studied narcissism agree that narcissistic behavior can often mask feelings of self-doubt and inferiority. The narcissist has a weak sense of self and attempts to compensate for this by engaging in grandiose fantasies and by seeking admiration and approval from others (Masterson 7–9). As Richard M. Restak states in his book *The Self Seekers*, "For the narcissist, life consists of an unending round of maneuvers aimed at bolstering self-esteem" (128). So long as these maneuvers are successful, the narcissist gives the appearance of being extremely self-satisfied. If, however, these maneuvers fail, the narcissist's feelings of self-doubt well up, resulting in severe depression.

Toad's periodic bouts with depression clearly follow this pattern. He tries to think of himself as an admired figure, but when this image is threatened he becomes despondent. The most dramatic example of this type of reaction occurs when Toad is imprisoned. Faced with a lengthy sentence, he practically loses his will to live. He refuses his meals, and he constantly castigates himself. At one point he calls himself a "stupid animal" and then goes on to say, "Now I must languish in this dungeon, till people who were proud to say they knew me, have forgotten the very name of Toad" (142–43). His depression, in other words, stems from his realization that he may have lost the admiration of his peers. He comes out of his depression only after having convinced himself that the jailer's daughter "admired him very much" (147).

In addition to causing depression, the narcissist's sense of self-doubt can lead to other problems. One of these is a tendency to engage in dangerous activities. Restak provides the following explanation for this behavior:

> Burdened with crushing feelings of inertia and deadness, the understimulated self frantically reaches out to the world in order to grasp the excitement and vitality which it inwardly lacks. Forms of self-stimulation replace natural and spontaneous excitements. Frantic efforts are employed to critically stir up a sense of aliveness and

vitality. Addictions, sexual promiscuity and perversions, alcohol
and drug-induced "highs," dangerous sports and recreational activities (hang gliding, motorcycle racing, etc.)—all are, in the last
analysis, attempts to artificially repair the chronic state of under-
stimulation [108].

The urge to live recklessly is certainly present in Toad. He feels that
he is "at his best and highest" (121) when he is careening around in an automobile. He finds it impossible to drive at a moderate speed, even though
he knows that he is risking his life. In fact, the knowledge that he is in danger gives Toad a sense of exhilaration. Such behavior may also be indica-
tive of subconscious self-destructive impulses. The fact that he continues
to drive recklessly after being injured in several accidents suggests that, on
some level, Toad's accidents are deliberate. According to Karl Menninger,
an authority on self-destructive behavior, such purposive accidents are a
step in the direction of suicide (293–94). It is possible, in other words, that
Toad's self-doubt borders on self-negation.

Since the narcissist is preoccupied with himself, he has difficulty relat-
ing to others. This point is stressed in the original Narcissus myth. Handsome Narcissus is sought after by many would-be lovers, but he rejects their
advances. Instead, he falls in love with his own reflection. Contemporary
theorists argue that the narcissist is incapable of forming strong bonds
with others largely because of an inability to feel empathy. While the narcissist may be gregarious, he is primarily interested in winning admiration
from others, not their friendship or love. Expanding on this point, Restak
explains that "people are important to the narcissist only as a means of bolstering his sense of self" (128).

The narcissist's approach to relationships characterizes Toad's dealings
with Mole, Rat and Badger. Toad is always a gracious host, but he refuses
to talk about anything but himself. He constantly boasts about his posses-
sions and embraces anyone who seems to admire his things. He takes an
instant liking to Mole, for example, simply because Mole is impressed
with his new caravan. Toad never concerns himself with how his actions
might adversely affect others, and he shows little gratitude when his friends
attempt to help him. Although they have come to expect such behavior,
Toad's friends are sometimes hurt by his lack of empathy. Toward the end
of the book, Rat tells Toad, "You don't deserve to have such true and loyal
friends, Toad, you don't really" (225). Toad begins apologizing to Rat, but
he stops in mid-sentence upon learning that supper is ready.

The narcissist's inability to accept other people as equals results in
another problem—an inability to accept criticism. In the opinion of the

narcissist, no one has a right to criticize his behavior; anyone who does is perceived as being cruel and unreasonable. Nathan Schwartz-Salant discusses this narcissistic trait in *Narcissism and Character Transformation*:

> The experience of being with a person with a narcissistic character disorder is one of being kept away, warded off…. Criticism is met with extreme resistance. The person with a narcissistic character disorder has so little sense of identity … that any criticism at all is felt as a personal threat [37–38].

Toad's resistance to criticism is evident throughout *The Wind in the Willows*. On numerous occasions, Badger and Rat criticize Toad for his selfish and self-destructive behavior, but Toad never recognizes the legitimacy of their complaints. He sometimes gives the appearance of making constructive use of criticism, but he immediately reverts to his old ways. For instance, when Badger criticizes Toad for driving so recklessly, Toad apologizes and promises to reform. A few minutes later, however, he says, "I've been searching my mind since, and going over things in it, and I find that I'm not a bit sorry or repentant really, so it's no earthly good saying I am" (110). Since Toad seems to be incapable of accepting criticism, his apparent reform at the end of the book is unconvincing. One wonders why Toad is suddenly able to respond constructively to criticism. Grahame was well aware of this problem. In response to an inquiry about Toad's transformation, Grahame wrote, "Of course Toad never really reformed; he was by nature incapable of it. But the subject is a painful one to pursue" (Grahame, *My Dearest Mouse* 190).

Although Toad can be seen as having a narcissistic personality disorder, it is more difficult to explain why he developed this problem. Psychologists are not in complete agreement about the causes of narcissistic behavior in adults. In recent years, however, Heinz Kohut's theories on this subject have gained a considerable following. Kohut argues that the young child has a fragile but grandiose sense of selfhood. This fragile self can easily disintegrate unless it is reinforced. Most parents, Kohut believes, achieve this reinforcement by accepting and confirming the child's sense of self in all of its grandiosity. As Michael J. Patton and John S. Sullivan state in an article on Kohut's theories, most parents help their child "believe that he or she is perfect, powerful, loved, admired, and in symbiotic union with others" (376). Kohut calls this process mirroring (116). If this mirroring process does not occur, Kohut feels that the child may never develop a secure sense of self. Such a child, upon reaching adulthood, is likely to become a narcissist.

Grahame provides little information about Toad's childhood, but the information he does provide suggests that Toad may not have experienced the mirroring process that Kohut describes. At no point in the book is Toad's mother mentioned while Toad's father is mentioned on several occasions. Thus Toad's mother may not have been available to help build her son's sense of self. Toad's father was present, but he may have been too preoccupied to pay much attention to his son.

The elder Toad clearly spent most of his time amassing his fortune and maintaining Toad Hall. He also showed little confidence in his son. He never, for example, told his son about the underground passage into Toad Hall. According to Badger, he felt that Toad was too "light and volatile in character" (230) to be entrusted with the secret. It is possible, therefore, that Toad never experienced the unequivocal acceptance of a loving parent. This lack of parental acceptance may explain why, as an adult, Toad so desperately seeks approval and admiration.

Although this interpretation of Toad's personality explains much of his behavior, some may feel that it robs Toad of his charm. Toad is dearly loved by countless readers, and it is hard to accept the psychological problems of a loved one even if he is only a fictional character. Psychiatrists and psychologists are well aware of this difficulty. Often the friends of a psychiatric patient initially refuse to acknowledge their friend's problems. Once they do, they tend to distance themselves from their friend.

Such reactions are understandable, but they do a disservice to their friend. It is important to acknowledge a friend's psychological problems, but it is also important to remember the friend's endearing qualities. This holds true for Toad as well. He is a narcissist, but he is also an amusing companion. He is gregarious and often generous. His childish antics are amusing, and his exuberant approach to life is stimulating. Even though he may not be capable of truly loving others, there is something lovable about Toad. He longs for company, and it would be a shame if the acknowledgment of his narcissistic tendencies cost him his friends.

Works Cited

Freud, Sigmund. "On Narcissism." In vol. 14 of *The Standard Edition of the Complete Psychological Works of Sigmund Freud*. Trans. James Strachey. 24 vols. London: Hogarth, 1957.

Grahame, Elspeth. Introduction. *First Whisper of "The Wind in the Willows."* By Kenneth Grahame. Ed. Elspeth Grahame. 1–22. Philadelphia: Lippincott, 1945.

Grahame, Kenneth. *My Dearest Mouse: "The Wind in the Willows" Letters*. Ed. Marilyn Watts. London: Pavilion, 1988.

_____. *The Wind in the Willows*. New York: Scribner's, 1965.

Green, Peter. *Kenneth Grahame: A Biography*. Cleveland: World, 1959.

Hamilton, Victoria. *Narcissus and Oedipus: The Children of Psychoanalysis*. London: Routledge and Kegan Paul, 1982.

Kohut, Heinz. *The Analysis of the Self*. New York: International Universities, 1971.

Kuznets, Lois R. *Kenneth Grahame*. Boston: Twayne, 1987.

Masterson, James F. *The Narcissistic and Borderline Disorders*. New York: Brunner/Mazel, 1981.

Menninger, Karl. *Man Against Himself*. New York: Harcourt, 1938.

Patton, Michael J. and John J. Sullivan. "Heinz Kohut and the Classical Psychoanalytic Tradition: An Analysis in Terms of Levels of Explanation." *Psychoanalytic Review* 64 (1980): 365–88.

Restak, Richard M. *The Self Seekers*. Garden City, New York: Doubleday, 1982.

Schwartz-Salant, Nathan. *Narcissism and Character Transformation: The Psychology of Narcissistic Character Disorders*. Toronto: Inner City, 1982.

Tucker, Nicholas. "The Children's Falstaff." *Suitable for Children: Controversies in Children's Literature*. Ed. Nicholas Tucker. 160–64. Berkeley: University of California Press, 1976.

CHAPTER 5

The Reproduction of Mothering in *Charlotte's Web*

Lucy Rollin

Nancy Chodorow's signal study *The Reproduction of Mothering* (1978), taking its cue from psychoanalytic object relations theory, argues that in our culture girls' relationships with their mothers are more intense, ambivalent, and lingering than those with their fathers. Because she is nurtured by a parent of the same sex, a daughter retains her mother as primary object throughout adolescence and into adulthood. This helps perpetuate the division of labor in our society: although theoretically both girls and boys are psychologically capable of mothering, both having after all *been* mothered, only girls in fact do it. Hence the "reproduction" of mothering—its continuation from mother to daughter. Chodorow carefully distinguishes psychological processes of reproduction from role training or intentional socialization:

> In an industrial late capitalist society, "socialization" is a particularly psychological affair.... Whether or not men in particular or society at large—through media, income distribution, welfare policies, and schools—enforce women's mothering, and expect or require a woman to care for her child, they cannot require or force her to provide adequate parenting unless she, *to some degree and on some unconscious or conscious level*, has the capacity and sense of self as maternal to do so [32–33].

According to Chodorow, mothering in our culture is part of an economic system that contributes to sexual inequality and that relies above all on internalized gender distinctions.

Part of the fascination of E.B. White's *Charlotte's Web* comes from its insertion of a male into the chain of mothering among the book's females. The novel offers an innovative picture of mothering that seems to belie internalized gender distinctions and to suggest that males are indeed as capable of mothering as females. Moreover, whereas Chodorow seems to slight the importance of physiology, *Charlotte's Web* subtly allows physical mothering to share the focus with psychological mothering, enhancing the complexity of the depiction. Yet significant differences between male and female mothering, coupled with the pressure of gender stereotypes in the narrative, suggest a reading of the novel that supports Chodorow's assertions about mothering as a psychological activity of females. This reading also raises important questions about gender and mothering in our culture and about the influence of a work of literature—especially a work of children's literature—on our attitudes toward them.[1]

The first transmission of mothering appears in the opening pages of the book. Having saved the life of a runt piglet, whom she names Wilbur, Fern learns from her mother how to care for her new charge:

> Mrs. Arable found a baby's nursing bottle and a rubber nipple. She poured warm milk into the bottle, fitted the nipple over the top, and handed it to Fern. "Give him his breakfast," she said.
> A minute later, Fern was seated on the floor in the corner of the kitchen with her infant between her knees, teaching it to suck from the bottle [5–7].

There could hardly be a more graphic example of the reproduction of mothering than this. Here and in the following pages, Fern's relationship to Wilbur typifies the initial phase of the mutual involvement and identification between mother and child: they worship each other. Fern thinks it is a "blissful world" because she has "entire charge of a pig"; she gets up early in the morning to feed him and rushes home from school to fix another bottle for him, and when she watches him in the straw, "it relieved her mind to know that her baby would sleep covered up, and would stay warm" (9). For his part, Wilbur gazes at Fern "with adoring eyes" and follows her everywhere. Throughout this phase, feeding and touch are of the utmost importance in mothering. Both elements are essential for an infant's primary narcissism, which Wilbur experiences fully: "Every day was a happy day, and every night was peaceful" (11).

But mothering relationships are essentially asymmetrical. As Chodorow notes, a child's relationship to its mother is exclusive, whereas a mother's to her child is informed by many other concerns. Fern must go to school, leaving Wilbur behind each day, and eventually she must send

Wilbur to the Zuckerman farm. This partial separation causes Wilbur his first anxiety: "He didn't feel like going to sleep, he didn't feel like digging, he was tired of standing still, tired of lying down. 'I'm less than two months old and I'm tired of living,' he said" (16). His loneliness overcomes him often, and he feels "friendless, dejected, and hungry" because his needs for touch and food are no longer so easily gratified.

Wilbur remains aware of Fern, knowing "she was sitting there, right outside his pen" (16). She has become his internalized object, associated with food and touch, the "first" mother that always exists somewhere in our unconscious. The shift in the narrative structure at this point in the book expresses this subtle relationship very well. Fern gradually disappears from Wilbur's conscious life to be replaced often by food, especially milk, but the blissful combination of food and touch exists for him now only in Mrs. Zuckerman's buttermilk baths. Fern's withdrawal causes him pain and may puzzle some readers (especially when at the end of the book she goes off with Henry Fussy), but it is psychologically essential both for Fern and for Wilbur.[2] Fern must develop her own outside interests, just as her own mother has done, and though they frustrate the child's desire to re-create its first intimacy and sense of merging, they are essential if the child is to form a self—that is, an identity separate from the mother (Chodorow 70–71, 79–80).

As Fern recedes from mother figure to internalized object, Charlotte the spider takes over the mothering of Wilbur—a different form of mothering. Charlotte and Wilbur never touch each other, and Charlotte never feeds Wilbur. She accomplishes her mothering solely through language. She advises, scolds, compliments, sings lullabies, tells stories, and finally weaves words into her web—attentions Wilbur accepts passively at first. Indeed, the novel's references to Charlotte and Wilbur as "friends" probably results from the absence of touch and feeding in their relationship, but Charlotte is no less a mother object.

Their meeting begins pleasantly enough, with Wilbur thinking Charlotte "beautiful" and Charlotte agreeing. Soon, however, she is capturing and devouring a fly in her web and explaining her actions in detail to Wilbur, who watches "in horror." Describing her insect diet, she says she loves to "drink their blood." She adds, "My mother was a trapper before me. Her mother was a trapper before her," and notes further that "the first spider in the early days of the world" was female (39–40). Wilbur, after all this, finds her "fierce, brutal, scheming, bloodthirsty.... How can I learn to like her?" This new mother offers love and acceptance, but also danger and risk. Can he trust her as he trusted Fern? "When a person's early experience tells

him or her that only one unique person can provide emotional gratifica-
tions—a realistic expectation when they have been intensely and exclusively
mothered—the desire to recreate that experience has to be ambivalent"
(Chodorow 79).

The text emphasizes Charlotte's indulgent fondness for Wilbur: she
expresses affection for him, makes plans for his future, tells him she likes
him best when he is "not a quitter," scolds his extravagant behavior, and
tells him he is sensational. But the greatest threat a mother offers is aban-
donment. Like Fern, Charlotte gradually withdraws, becoming more interested in her egg sac, and eventually becomes more voice than physical
presence. Here again, the text shows the asymmetry that marks our culture's form of mothering.

With Charlotte's death and Wilbur's acquisition of her egg sac, the
reproduction of mothering shifts gender: now Wilbur mothers. This
moment also marks a shift in focus from postnatal to prenatal care. Wilbur
rises to the demands of parenthood by sacrificing food to secure the help
of Templeton, a shifty male, protectively carrying the egg sac in his mouth
(in imitation of gestation), scooping out a special place for it, guarding and
warming it with his breath on cold nights.[3] He takes much pride and pleasure in all this: "Life is always a rich and steady time when you are waiting for something to happen or hatch" (176). This must be one of the most
appealing moments in the book for children, who try to imagine what their
mothers were like before they were born, since these internalized images
of pregnancy reinforce the importance of their own birth and protection.

The sac containing Charlotte's babies also becomes a representation
of oedipal desire. Wilbur had commented with pride earlier to Templeton, "She is going to become a mother. For your information there are 514
eggs in that peachy little sac." Immediately after this, the text tells us that
Charlotte and Wilbur were "glad to be rid of" Templeton when he went
to sleep (149). Wilbur's hyperbolic 514 babies not only occasion pride and
possessiveness but totally diffuse any sibling rivalries. Moreover, while
Wilbur ensures Charlotte's survival in her children, through those (female)
children who stay with him he ensures his own survival as well.

Allied to this oedipal fantasy is the fantasy of redemption from death.
Although psychoanalytic theory has not often addressed the issue in detail,
it assumes that the desire to give birth occurs in both boys and girls, finding
this desire "historically older" than the phallic stage and marked especially
in the male by a strong unconscious fear of death (Jacobson 144–45). The
text astutely uses a pig to express this fear, since our culture keeps pigs
solely to slaughter and eat them and thus justifies Wilbur's fear.

More interestingly, the child's desire to give birth "even seems to reflect, at first, only the mother-child situation without involving fantasies about the relationship between the parents" (Jacobson 141). The fantasy reproduction in this text is asexual: Charlotte has no visible male partner. This is an infantile fantasy for both boys and girls, though Chodorow suggests it may be stronger and more complex in girls. "On a less conscious, object-relational level, having a child recreates the desired mother-child exclusivity for a woman, and interrupts it for a man.... These differences hold also on the level of sexual and biological fantasy and symbolism" (Chodorow 201).

Once the spiders hatch, Wilbur's mothering differs even further from that by the females. He does name the spiders as Fern named him, and he mothers with words, as Charlotte did. Fern and Charlotte, however, move on to other kinds of lives, Charlotte to reproduction and Fern to adolescence. Wilbur, by contrast, at the end of the book has returned to essentially the same state he was in at the beginning: basking in the daily care of the Zuckermans, the companionship of the other animals, and the completely undemanding "friendship" of the little female spiders. For him, life "was very good—night and day, winter and summer, spring and fall, dull days and bright days. It was the best place to be" (183). Moreover, although he loves Charlotte's children and grandchildren, none of them "ever quite took her place in his heart" (184). Wilbur's "mother," loving and dangerous, remains his dominant attachment.

Wilbur's mothering, then, differs from Mrs. Arable's, Fern's, and Charlotte's in the degree of its grounding in infantile fantasy. It represents unusually complicated wish fulfillment: oedipal desire for the mother, participation in pregnancy, asexual reproduction, exaggerated multiple birth, redemption from death, a continuing dependent and narcissistic state, assurance that such a state will never end, and finally the maintenance of the mother as primary love object.

Mothering in females can also represent such wish fulfillment, but in the book Wilbur provides the focus for it. His condition at the end of the book reflects the fundamental asymmetry of daily reproduction: "Men are socially and psychologically reproduced by women, but women are reproduced (or not) largely by themselves" (Chodorow 36). The little spiders, all females, reproduce themselves generation after generation; Wilbur's life has been entirely reproduced by the females around him.

Chodorow emphasizes that mothering is only one role that females play in our culture, albeit a major one and one strongly encouraged by the culture. But the end of *Charlotte's Web* suggests that mothering is the only active role that Wilbur will ever play in life. Having re-created his exclu-sive primary attachment to his mother, he needs to do nothing further. This is certainly powerful fantasy material, for child and adult readers of both sexes, but if Wilbur's maleness was significant in his mothering duties, it must also be significant in this ending. The final image of him in the com-fortable barn, childlike and happy, comes very close to the stereotype of the childlike, dependent husband. The difference is that Wilbur does not fear this state of dependency, as Chodorow suggests many men do (199).

The novel depicts other male stereotypes as well, and much less pleas-ant ones. The first three pages of the book equate maleness with violence: Mr. Arable is about to kill the pig with an ax, and Avery, Fern's ten-year-old brother, appears "heavily armed—an air rifle in one hand, a wooden dag-ger in the other" (4). Mr. Arable's reason for the slaughter is that "a weakling makes trouble." Though he seems "almost ready to cry" when Fern protests the killing, he says, "I'll let you start it on a bottle, like a baby. Then you'll see what trouble a pig can be" (3)—the implication being that babies and weaklings are equal in their potential to make trouble. Avery's mother says her son is perfectly normal because he "gets into poison ivy and gets stung by wasps and bees and brings frogs and snakes home and breaks everything he lays his hands on. He's fine" (111–112).

Templeton, the only other male character who appears with regular-ity, is Wilbur's rival for food.[4] Dr. Dorian, who does allow the possibility of animal speech and thus speaks for the power of the imagination, nonetheless reinforces gender stereotypes with his patriarchal advice; his response to Mrs. Arable's complaint about Avery getting stung by wasps and bringing home snakes and breaking everything is a resounding and unequivocal "Good!" (112). The choice of the name Henry Fussy for the male who woos Fern seems calculated to make him less than attractive. It is also worth noting that Wilbur has no perceptible father.

By contrast, *Charlotte's Web* contains an unusual number of nurturing female characters. Some of them are as stereotyped as the men: the goose, Mrs. Arable, and Mrs. Zuckerman with her cleansing (and to Wilbur, deli-cious) buttermilk baths all tend to express stereotypical attitudes and behav-ior. Even Fern's attitudes do not quite escape the stereotype, especially as she moves into adolescence. But the sheer number of different mothers, of varying species, and all circulating around Wilbur, suggests the complexity of the mother image itself: a biological, psychological, spiritual, economic, social, and cultural construct which eludes full description and for which Charlotte's web is the perfect emblem. Charlotte reflects on the significance of web-building in the following exchange that she has with Wilbur:

"Not many creatures can spin webs. Even men aren't as good at it as spiders, although they *think* they're pretty good, and they'll *try* anything. Did you ever hear of the Queensborough Bridge?"

Wilbur shook his head. "Is it a web?"

"Sort of," replied Charlotte. "But do you know how long it took men to build it? Eight whole years.... I can make a web in a single evening."

"But what do people catch in the Queensborough Bridge—bugs?"

"They don't catch anything. They just keep trotting back and forth across the bridge thinking there is something better on the other side ... with men it's rush, rush every minute.... I know a good thing when I see it, and my web is a good thing" [60–61].

In Charlotte's eyes, a bridge is a bipolar thing allowing only two directions: back and forth. And while "men" may refer to human beings in general, Charlotte continually uses the word in a derogatory way here. A web, on the other hand, is a natural product allowing complex interactions in many directions; it represents the female Charlotte herself and her nurturing activities.

Drawing upon Chodorow's findings, Carol Gilligan has further explored the symbol of the web to represent women's notions of relationships; in her theory, women perceive relationships as a complex network of responsibility. They therefore often score poorly on psychological tests to elicit moral attitudes that are oriented toward a hierarchical image of relationships, for which an accurate image is the ladder. Each of these images—web and ladder—"distorts the other's representation. As the top of the hierarchy becomes the edge of the web and as the center of the network of connection becomes the middle of a hierarchical progression, each image marks as dangerous the place which the other defines as safe" (Gilligan 62). Males tend to fear being caught in a web of relationship and often respond to this possibility with fantasies of violence (39–42). Women, by contrast, fear being alone at the top of a hierarchy without the network of support which reproduces them (43–44).

Charlotte, however, knows no fear. As confident in the center of her web as she is at the top of the hierarchy of the barnyard animals, she escapes female stereotyping by combining masculine with feminine traits. Her scheming, trapping, bloodthirsty nature coexists with peaceful nurturance. The text describes her as "bold" and "cruel" (41), yet she draws support from her relationships with her female ancestors, her cousins, Wilbur, and the other animals.

Language, in the dichotomy between nature and culture, is usually associated with culture and hence with maleness. Yet Charlotte is both "a good friend and a good writer" (184). Janice Alberghene has described the importance of writing in *Charlotte's Web*, noting that Charlotte teaches Wilbur about language and its use by weaving words as she weaves her web. Just as language is frequently tied to male culture, weaving allies itself with the female (see especially Rowe). But Charlotte breaks down these dichotomies, incorporating in one body, and in her web, the nurturing voice of the female and the cultural voice of the male. She becomes, virtually, the perfect parent.

This valorization of motherhood is one of the most appealing aspects of *Charlotte's Web* and encourages a reading in which gender distinctions are erased. However, just as Wilbur's maleness cannot be entirely ignored, so Charlotte's femaleness is stressed throughout the book and remains central to her nurturing. From this point of view, the novel supports Chodorow's contention that our culture socializes women to become mothers, based on psychological as well as physical criteria—that is, by emphasizing internalized gender distinctions. In *Charlotte's Web* the reproduction of mothering, despite a male's temporary participation, remains the province of the female.

The phenomenal popularity of *Charlotte's Web* in this country was recently confirmed by a "Reading Is Fundamental" survey, which asked eighty "celebrities" and nearly 750,000 schoolchildren to name their favorite children's book. *Charlotte's Web* scored high among the children, and celebrities Ann Landers and Erma Bombeck (who "mother" thousands through the popular press) named it as their special favorite, as did numerous teachers, librarians, and parents who are RIF volunteers (*Greenville* [SC] *News*, 2A). Such widespread popularity indicates that the depiction of motherhood in this book corresponds to the desires and fantasies of a large and varied population, who find in it much that is comforting. This comforting quality raises questions, though, about gender and nurturing in our culture today.

Wilbur's passivity at the end of the book certainly provides a comforting fantasy—especially for a child reader, since it implies that happiness and peace need not be associated solely with maturity and action or with the evolving gender distinctions that seem to accompany maturity. But it also implies the possibility of replicating the mother-child bond without involving a father and suggests that, while the female nurturing characters in the book must grow and change, the chief male one need not. Chodorow believes that such a fantasy would not be disturbing to girls, since girls do not define themselves by denying pre-oedipal relational modes (167). Boys, however, must relinquish those modes to achieve mature masculinity. What is the effect of such a literary fantasy, then, on boys? It would be interesting to discover if *Charlotte's Web* affects boys differently from girls.[5]

Charlotte's complexity and the valorization of motherhood, through her and her web, must certainly provide comfort and even inspiration to readers, especially female ones. Moreover, this book focuses entirely on the domestic sphere, where the world of men gives way to women—to women's use of language and women's relationships. Furthermore, the main character, a male, is central to the web of the text because he is central to the web of female relationships that structure it. However, Chodorow reminds us of social realities in our culture:

> Women's mothering determines women's primary location in the domestic sphere and creates a basis for the structural differentiation of domestic and public spheres. But these spheres operate hierarchically. Kinship rules organize claims of men on domestic units, and men dominate kinship. Culturally and politically, the public sphere dominates the domestic, and hence men dominate women [10].

The women seem dominant in this novel; yet their power reaches only a little beyond the domestic (to the county fair) and Mrs. Arable must turn to an unmistakable patriarchal figure, Dr. Dorian, for advice about her daughter's imagination. Thus, while the fantasy of the novel seems to valorize motherhood, it does so within a tightly controlled domain. Might this subtle aspect of such a popular novel not in some way contribute to keeping women in the domestic sphere?

Finally, the stereotypes in the book also offer both positive and negative comfort. Readers may smile at Avery's foolishness in acting like a pig, or at Mrs. Arable's narrow-minded equation of crocheting with web-spinning, or at her encouragement of Henry Fussy's attentions to Fern, recognizing that such behavior is only part of the truth. Indeed, these stereotypes emerge so clearly in *Charlotte's Web* because they are juxtaposed with the unstereotypical behavior of Wilbur and Charlotte.

Still, even in as fine and complex a novel as this, stereotypes may feed fears. For example, do the characters of the "heavily armed" Avery, the ax-carrying Mr. Arable, and the devouring Templeton reflect women's fear of men's potential for violence? How might boys react to hearing such depictions read to them by their female teachers or mothers? If this novel suggests that men are indeed capable of mothering, might not such accompanying depictions, especially in a children's book, delay societal and personal changes? Given the remarkable dissemination of this novel across ages, races, and classes in this country, these are significant questions.

Charlotte's Web has the power to affect readers deeply on many issues. Relatively few people will read Nancy Chodorow's theories, but *Charlotte's Web* anticipated her exploration of gender and motherhood with its complex interweaving of stereotype and innovation, depicting motherhood as both a biological and a psychological process that rests, in our culture, finally with the female. In so doing, it has provided various forms of comfort for countless readers.

As our society tries to break down gender distinctions with regard to nurturing, the underlying gender distinctions that inform this novel take on even greater importance. They are not a mere relic of 1952, when the novel first appeared, but, as Chodorow shows, a sign of something deeply ingrained, unconscious, and thus all the more powerful in us. They cannot be overcome until they are recognized—especially in as fine and influential a book as White's *Charlotte's Web*.

Notes

1. In this essay, I treat *Charlotte's Web* as a text; addressing questions of psychobiography would entail a different psychoanalytical approach, but the authorship of this hymn to motherhood by a male, E.B. White, would provide the focus for an interesting study in itself.

2. Perry Nodelman describes this shift from "innocence" to "experience" as one from naturalism to fantasy (126). The two-part structure is not pure, though; later sections in the novel are in the "naturalistic" mode. Object relations theory helps us to see why Fern must be encouraged by her mother, in naturalistic passages, to develop a "normal" interest in boys (104–11), and how she remains an internalized mother for Wilbur at the point of transition to the fantastic.

3. From an anthropological point of view, such male activity is not unusual, of course. Many cultures practice various forms of couvade, and the rite is regarded as a useful, even essential element in the birth practice. Until recently, modern Western culture denied men such rites and fantasies, reducing them to pacing in the hospital waiting room.

4. Young readers' enjoyment of Templeton may be explained psychoanalytically in part; while Wilbur remains generally in the oral stage, Templeton with his hoarding and overconsumption is a much more anal character. Wilbur eats, but Templeton devours. Young children are chronologically and psychologically much closer to their own anality than most adults and thus less likely to find it unattractive.

5. It would also be interesting to discover whether *Charlotte's Web* is more or less popular among boys than girls. In the RIF survey, the book was named by children as a favorite "along with other books." No male celebrity cited in the article named the book, but the "teachers, librarians and parents" who are RIF volunteers named the book overwhelmingly as a favorite. That the "great majority" of these volunteers are female was confirmed by a phone conversation with RIF headquarters (June 27, 1989).

Works Cited

Alberghene, Janice. "Writing in *Charlotte's Web.*" *Children's Literature in Education* (Spring 1985): 32–44.

"Celebrities Tell What They Liked to Read When They Were Young." AP wire service. *Greenville* (SC) *News*, 30 March 1987, 2A.

Chodorow, Nancy. *The Reproduction of Mothering.* Berkeley: University of California Press, 1978.

Gilligan, Carol. *In a Different Voice.* Cambridge: Harvard University Press, 1982.

Jacobson, Edith. "Development of the Wish for a Child in Boys." *The Psychoanalytic Study of the Child* 5 (1950): 139–52.

Nodelman, Perry. "Text as Teacher: The Beginning of *Charlotte's Web.*" *Children's Literature* 13 (1985): 109–27.

Rowe, Karen E. "To Spin a Yarn: The Female Voice in Folklore and Fairy Tale." In *Fairy Tales and Society.* Ed. Ruth Bottigheimer. 53–74. Philadelphia: University of Pennsylvania Press, 1986.

White, E. B. *Charlotte's Web.* 1952. New York: Harper's, 1980.

CHAPTER 6

Pinocchio's Journey from the Pleasure Principle to the Reality Principle

Mark I. West

Before analyzing Pinocchio's psychological development, one must specify which Pinocchio is being put on the couch, for, as several critics have pointed out, there are two Pinocchios. The first Pinocchio was created by Carlo Collodi in the 1880s. The other Pinocchio was created by Disney in the late 1930s. While they share several surface characteristics, their personalities differ in significant ways. Collodi's Pinocchio is a more forceful, willful, and mischievous character than the Disney creation.[1] The two Pinocchios also take different paths toward psychological maturity.

In the Disney film, Pinocchio's psychological development is guided by Jiminy Cricket, a character who is loosely based on a minor figure in Collodi's book. In addition to being Pinocchio's constant companion, Jiminy Cricket serves as Pinocchio's moral mentor. He informs Pinocchio of his moral obligations, gently criticizes him when he misbehaves, and praises him when he behaves properly. Jiminy Cricket, in other words, can be seen as a personified superego. Jiminy Cricket continues to take care of his charge until Pinocchio's own superego is firmly established. This change occurs during the film's conclusion. Soon after Pinocchio is turned into a real boy, Jiminy Cricket tells Pinocchio to "always let your conscience be your guide." Pinocchio responds by saying, "Yes, sir, I will!"

Collodi's Pinocchio, unlike his Disney counterpart, has no omnipresent adviser to guide him. Although he encounters a number of characters who give him moralistic advice, he generally regards their words of wisdom as worthless poppycock. Still, he does mature over the course of the book. Initially he is an impulsive and lazy brat, but he becomes a patient and hard-working boy. This transformation, however, does not occur simply because Pinocchio has internalized a rigid superego. The process that Collodi uses to account for Pinocchio's transformation is more complex. In order to explain this process, it is helpful to refer to Freud's thoughts on the relationship between what he calls the pleasure principle and the reality principle.

Freud defines the pleasure principle as the instinctual drive to achieve pleasure and avoid unpleasure. This principle, according to Freud, can be used to describe the mental activity of very young children. He argues that this is why young children demand that their needs and wants be gratified immediately. Eventually, however, children learn that the pursuit of pleasure can sometimes have unpleasurable consequences. They learn that unless they take the external world into consideration, their attempts to achieve pleasure are likely to fail. Freud suggests that this discovery leads to the formation of the reality principle.[2] He elaborates on this idea in *Beyond the Pleasure Principle*:

> Under the influence of the ego's instincts of self-preservation, the pleasure principle is replaced by the reality principle. This latter principle does not abandon the intention of ultimately obtaining pleasure, but it nevertheless demands and carries into effect the postponement of satisfaction, the abandonment of a number of possibilities of gaining satisfaction and the temporary toleration of unpleasure as a step on the long indirect road to pleasure [10].

In the beginning of Collodi's book, Pinocchio behaves in accordance with the pleasure principle. Not only does he demand food and entertainment, but he also enjoys acting out his aggressive impulses. One of the first things that he does after coming into being is kick Geppetto in the nose. When Geppetto or anyone else suggests that he do anything that he views as being unpleasurable, such as attending school, he steadfastly refuses. Both Geppetto and the talking cricket tell him that he is misbehaving, but their criticisms do not cause him to act differently. Throughout the first six chapters, he impulsively pursues pleasure without giving any serious thought to the consequences of his actions.

Pinocchio's behavior starts to change in the seventh chapter. This change is not the result of a moral awakening on the part of Pinocchio.

Rather, it is tied to Pinocchio's growing awareness of the external world. After a fruitless search for food, he discovers that he needs the help of others if he is to eat. He becomes even more aware of his need for help after his feet are "burned away to cinders" (33). This problem arose because he had attempted to dry his cold wet feet by placing them on a hot brazier. His need for food and new feet forces Pinocchio to think about his relationship with Geppetto. He begins to realize that he is dependent on the same man whom he had earlier kicked in the nose. One consequence of this is that he starts to change his behavior. Instead of kicking Geppetto, he now gives him hugs. This change occurs primarily because Pinocchio is beginning to follow the dictates of the reality principle.

As the reality principle begins to exert itself, Pinocchio's attitude toward school changes. Although he still dislikes the idea of going to school, he expresses a willingness to attend. He decides that he would rather endure the displeasurable aspects of going to school than risk alienating Geppetto. He also thinks that the information that he will learn will enable him to attain pleasure in the future. While walking to school, he fantasizes about this point. "Today," he tells himself, "I shall learn to read in no time; tomorrow I shall learn to write, and the day after tomorrow I shall learn all the figures. Then I shall be clever enough to earn lots of money" (43). There is, however, a tentative quality to Pinocchio's decision to attend school. He still is strongly influenced by the pleasure principle, and as a result he is easily distracted when pleasurable temptations present themselves.

On his way to school, Pinocchio succumbs to two temptations which prevent him from reaching his destination. He sells his primer in order to watch a puppet show, and he participates in a get-rich scheme proposed to him by the cat and the fox. On both occasions, he discovers that yielding to the pleasure principle can have disastrous results. He is nearly burned to death by the fierce puppeteer, and the cat and the fox attempt to kill him by hanging him from a tree. Because of these experiences, Pinocchio begins to realize that he cannot afford to ignore the dictates of the reality principle. This lesson is made even clearer to Pinocchio soon after the blue fairy saves his life. She has him taken down from the tree where the cat and the fox had left him, but he remains near death. His only hope is to drink some foul tasting medicine. The part of his mind that is governed by the pleasure principle opts not to take the medicine in order to avoid the unpleasant taste. However, when the certainty of death becomes clear to Pinocchio, he acts in accordance with the reality principle and drinks the medicine.

Taking his medicine proves to be a turning point for Pinocchio, for soon after this incident he makes a significant break away from the pleasure principle. While he is being forced to serve as a peasant's watchdog, four polecats offer him a plucked chicken for breakfast so long as he does not inform the peasant when they raid the poultry yard. Although Pinocchio loves to eat, he turns down their offer and tells the peasant about the raid. This is the first time that he successfully resists a pleasurable temptation. The peasant rewards Pinocchio by giving him back his freedom. Thus, Pinocchio learns that defying the pleasure principle can sometimes result in future pleasure.

Another way in which Pinocchio moves beyond the pleasure principle is by actually attending school. He decides to go to school after the blue fairy promises to turn him into a real boy if he gives up his idle ways. He agrees to change, but he still does not see studying as a pleasurable activity. In announcing his decision to the blue fairy, he says, "School gives me a pain. But from this day forward, I shall turn over a new leaf" (133). Even though the other students harass him, he remains in school and eventually becomes an exemplary student.

Collodi describes him as being "attentive, studious, and intelligent, first to arrive at school, and the last to leave when school was over" (138). At one point he allows himself to be distracted from his studies, but he returns as an even more conscientious student. The blue fairy is so impressed with his good behavior that she begins making plans to turn him into a real boy.

Before Pinocchio can become a real boy, however, he must make one more break away from the pleasure principle. He must accept the necessity of working, an idea that he still finds repugnant. Pinocchio is certainly not the only person to face this problem. Since work at first appears to be unpleasurable, most people do not willingly engage in this activity unless their actions are governed primarily by the reality principle (Brill 136–138). This generally does not happen until the onset of adolescence. Adjusting to the reality of work is, according to Erik H. Erikson, one of the final tasks that a child must face before becoming a young adult. In describing the ideal way in which this transition occurs, Erikson writes:

> [The child] develops a sense of industry—i.e., he adjusts himself to the inorganic laws of the tool world. He can become an eager and absorbed unit of a productive situation. To bring a productive situation to completion is an aim which gradually supersedes the whims and wishes of play [259].

Although Pinocchio is a good student, he is not quite ready to make work a higher priority than play. This issue comes to a head when he is presented with an opportunity to go to Playland, a country where children "have nothing but fun from morning till night" (177). At first he resists this temptation, in part because he knows that he will not be turned into a real boy if he goes. In the end, though, he succumbs. He discovers, however, that leading the life of a perpetual child can have adverse results. It proves to be unrewarding, it isolates him from those who love him, and it eventually robs him of his identity. Fortunately, he recovers from this period of regression, and when he does, he is finally ready to take on adult responsibilities.

Immediately after his recovery, Pinocchio is swallowed by a gigantic shark. Once inside the shark, he meets Geppetto. Pinocchio leads Geppetto out of the shark and helps him reach the shore. Geppetto, however, is weak and in need of nourishment. Pinocchio asks a local resident for a cup of milk for Geppetto, but the man insists that he be paid for it. Since Pinocchio has no money, he agrees to turn a windlass for the man in return for the milk. This is the first time that Pinocchio voluntarily works. He continues to work for the man during the mornings, and he works as a basket weaver in the afternoons. Pinocchio becomes a diligent worker, and in so doing he proves that he is no longer a slave to the pleasure principle. He is now able to cope with reality.

Recognizing that Pinocchio has achieved a higher level of psychological maturity, the blue fairy finally turns him into a real boy. In actuality, though, he becomes a young adult, not a boy (Morrissey and Wunderlich, "Death and Rebirth" 74). By taking Pinocchio from infancy into adolescence, Collodi provides insights into how a child moves from the pleasure principle to the reality principle.

Psychoanalysts would describe this process as a shift in dominance from the id to the ego, for it is the ego that balances the demands of the id with the constraints imposed by reality. Other forces, of course, affect Pinocchio's psychological development, but it is significant that Collodi emphasizes the importance of the ego over the superego. Collodi makes it clear that Pinocchio must gain control over his impulses, but Collodi does not insist that Pinocchio be made to feel overly guilty or ashamed about these impulses. In this regard, Collodi's book differs dramatically from most moralistic children's books from the nineteenth century.

Notes

1. For more information about the differences between Collodi's book and Disney's film, see May 468–469; Morrissey and Wunderlich, "Desecration of *Pinocchio*" 205–212; and Street 45–57.

2. Freud wrote about the pleasure principle and the reality principle in *Beyond the Pleasure Principle* 7–61; "Formulations on the Two Principles of Mental Functioning" 218–226; and *Introductory Lectures on Psychoanalysis* 356–357.

Works Cited

Brill, A. A. *Basic Principles of Psychoanalysis*. Garden City, NY: Doubleday, 1949.

Collodi, Carlo. *Pinocchio*. Trans. E. Harden. Middlesex, England: Puffin, 1974.

Erikson, Erik H. *Childhood and Society*. 2nd ed. New York: Norton, 1963.

Freud, Sigmund. *Beyond the Pleasure Principle*. In vol. 18 of *The Standard Edition of the Complete Psychological Works of Sigmund Freud*. Trans. James Strachey. 7–64. 24 vols. London: Hogarth, 1955.

_____. "Formulations on the Two Principles of Mental Functioning." In vol. 12 of *The Standard Edition of the Complete Psychological Works of Sigmund Freud*. Trans. James Strachey. 218–226. 24 vols. London: Hogarth, 1958.

_____. *Introductory Lectures on Psychoanalysis, Part III*. In vol. 16 of *The Standard Edition of the Complete Psychological Works of Sigmund Freud*. Trans. James Strachey. 243–463. 24 vols. London: Hogarth, 1963.

May, Jill P. "Walt Disney's Interpretation of Children's Literature." In *Jump Over the Moon: Selected Professional Readings*. Eds. Pamela Petrick Barron and Jennifer Q. Burley. 461–472. New York: Holt, 1984.

Morrissey, Thomas and Richard Wunderlich. "Death and Rebirth in Pinocchio." *Children's Literature* 11 (1983): 64–75.

_____. "The Desecration of *Pinocchio* in the United States." *Horn Book* April 1982: 205–212.

Street, Douglas. "*Pinocchio*—From Picaro to Pipsqueak." In *Children's Novels and the Movies*. Ed. Douglas Street. 47–57. New York: Ungar, 1983.

CHAPTER 7

Gazing and Mirroring in
The Prince and the Pauper

Lucy Rollin

Most recent critical literature on Mark Twain's *The Prince and the Pauper* concentrates on its patriarchal themes. For example, J. D. Stahl notes that each boy has three fathers, a kind of "mythic trinity" who struggle for control over them; Jerry Griswold suggests that the novel, along with other American novels appearing at that time, deals at one level with America's withdrawal from its own European roots—its political patriarch. For him the book represents post-oedipal concerns of succession.

I would like to explore some of the novel's feminine motifs, reading it through the theories of Winnicott and Lacan, with emphasis on gazing, desiring, perceiving. And mirror-like, at the same time, I read Winnicott and Lacan through *The Prince and the Pauper*, discovering ways of understanding the complexity of their ideas, especially as they relate to mothering. This is a theme that recurs in my own critical work, for it gives me an opportunity to gaze into the mirror of literature at my own reflection, as both a mother and a child. The simultaneous sense of completion and longing I experience represents, for me, the chief seduction of children's literature.

The *Prince and the Pauper* is a book full of gazing. Its seminal moment is when Tom and Edward exchange clothes and stand "side by side before a great mirror, and lo, a miracle: there did not seem to have been any change made! They stared at each other, then at the glass, then at each other again"

(64). Howard T. Baetzhold offers a curious and telling misreading of this moment in his fine study *Mark Twain and John Bull*, when he comments that the boys "stand naked before the mirror." They do not in fact stand before the mirror and see their similarity until they have exchanged clothes, but the moment is so powerful that they seem to be psychically naked— recognizing Oneself and Other simultaneously.

Other moments of intense gazing punctuate the novel, many of them loving and gentle. At their first meeting, Tom's mother gazes on Edward, her "son," yearningly, through her rising tears, while Edward looks into her face and gently reassures her. Later, while he sleeps, she examines his face, startling him with a noise and noticing that he does not cover his face as Tom does in similar circumstances, realizing therefore that this is not really her son. Miles Hendon, too, regards Edward in his sleep, contemplating him with "kind and pitying interest" and touching his cheek and hair, pondering how to care for him.

When Edward finds his way to a farmhouse and is discovered by two little girls, they gaze intensely at him and then accept him at his word; their mother also watches as he performs household tasks in a kind of test of his nobility. At their first meeting, Henry's stern face softens as he gazes lovingly at his "son" Tom, taking Tom's face between his hands and looking there for some sign of recognition and returning reason. The Princesses Elizabeth and Jane observe Tom in his role as Edward with curiosity and then kindness. All of the courtiers are instructed to show no sign in their faces that Tom's behavior is strange, an order which they carry out admirably and gently. In the procession to the throne, Tom's mother emerges from the crowd, her "intense eyes riveted upon him," her face "transfigured with joy and love" as she recognizes her true son.

In the complex process of an infant's development, as Winnicott theorizes it, the mother's gaze is central (and Winnicott hastens to say that always he includes the father in this notion). As the baby looks at the mother, the mother looks back, and what does the baby see? If the mother is not engaged with the baby, if she is being only herself, the baby may see the mother's face, in which case she is not a mirror, and perception takes the place of apperception. As the good-enough mother looks at her baby, she becomes a mirror. To the baby, in Winnicott's deceptively simple language, "what she looks like is related to what she sees there" ("Mirror" 112).

The baby sees itself reflected in her face, and this is "the beginning of a significant exchange with the world, a two-way process in which self-enrichment alternates with the discovery of meaning in the world of seen things" (113). This process begins with the mother but includes the whole family, which continues to give back to the child images of itself, helping the child to feel real, to relate to objects as itself, and to have a self to return to in times of stress.

Tom and Edward both experience this process. As Tom's dreams of princedom, encouraged by the old priest, begin to transform him from a naturally good-hearted boy into someone wise and dignified, he becomes a respected oddity in his rat-infested slum, and in Twain's words "a hero to all who knew him except his family—these, only, saw nothing in him." His heart becomes bitter as he struggles with the discrepancy between the self he is and the self he sees reflected in his family. When he takes Edward's place, he finds a different reflection in Henry's loving gaze, in the accepting looks of Elizabeth and Jane, in the bland faces of the courtiers, and in the ecstatic faces of the crowds who surround his processions through London. He becomes truly wise, delivering Solomon-like judgments and gaining strength from the exercise of his authority. But in order to continue he must also push aside his mother who, in spite of her love for him, represents the family he is trying to rise above.

For Winnicott (and here he shows his Kleinian roots), rejection is part of this two-way process. The mother as object must be lost before it can be found and appreciated as separate and valuable. Winnicott once wrote a prose "poem" he thought represented the baby's nonverbal communication with the mother, and which well describes Tom's relationship with his mother: "I find you; You survive what I do to you as I come to recognize you as not-me; I use you; I forget you; But you remember me; I keep forgetting you; I lose you; I am sad" ("Communication" 103).

This sadness is the Kleinian desire for reparation, and a sign of psychic health. Tom's reparation is made before the court when he immediately acknowledges Edward as rightful king, uses his office and his cleverness to persuade others of the truth, and "flies to his mother" in the closing lines of the novel.

The opposite of Tom's, Edward's early life has given him dignity and confidence; although he lacked a mother, his father and his surroundings have encouraged his growth, and what he misses most in his experiences as a beggar is the reinforcing gaze of others. But he finds this in Miles Hendon, who obeys his imperious orders gently and kindly, responding to the boy's calm authority. Hendon becomes a mother to Edward, just as Henry mothers Tom, acting as mirror to the boy's natural grace. Such mirroring allows Edward to see the injustices around him, just as Tom does in the palace, and to become a kindly and mature king (in Twain's re-creation, anyway). He "continued to tell the story" of his experience, "and thus keep its sorrowful spectacles fresh in his memory and the springs of plenty replenished in his heart," thereby making his reparation to his whole kingdom.

Both boys, in a Winnicottian reading, experience the healthy result of the two-way process that is the child's ego development. Winnicott summarizes its history thus: "When I look, I am seen, so I exist. I can now afford to look and see. I now look creatively and what I apperceive I also perceive" ("Mirror" 114).

In Lacan's reformulation of the concept of ego development, the process is not so sunny. He postulates the mirror stage, occurring in a child between the ages of 6 and 18 months; it is a moment of recognition and joy. Having to this point perceived itself in its mother's gaze, it now perceives itself as whole and separate, a vision which organizes the world and allows the child to imagine that it has mastery over its body. Lacan views this moment of happy self-absorption as the beginning of ego, of a relationship with the world and its objects. But for Lacan, the moment is also illusion, imagination, the beginning of desire which cannot be fulfilled: "the mirror stage is a drama whose internal thrust is precipitated from insufficiency to anticipation—and which manufactures for the subject, caught up in the lure of a spatial identification, the succession of phantasies" that ultimately result in "the armor of an alienating identity" (Lacan 4). Tom's dissatisfaction with life in Offal Court and Edward's longing for mud between his toes bring the two to the realization that they are "so marvelously twinned." Standing before the mirror they experience the illusion of completeness; separated immediately thereafter, they feel lonely as never before, and continue through the rest of the novel desiring what they do not have, citizens of, as Miles Hendon calls it, the Kingdom of Dreams and Shadows. For, just as do love and hope, delusions also rest in the gaze. The intense gaze of the old hermit is unrestful, glittering, seeing only what it wants to see. Edith, unhappy wife of Miles Hendon's usurping brother, turns her "stony and frightened gaze" on Hendon's eyes and deliberately and untruthfully denies she knows him. Those who give money to the beggars are deluded by their fake sores and injuries; the beggars themselves are deluded by Edward's ragged appearance; the vast crowds who follow Tom's processions are misled by his grand appurtenances. Even the reader is subject to spectacle: Twain inserts several lengthy descriptions of royal procession and of violent rabble, so that we gaze too and may be beguiled by what we "see": "We tingle to our fingertips with the electric thrill that is shot through us by the surprise and beauty of the spectacle!" says Twain, even when the spectacle is centered on a falsehood. Of course, Twain underscores the irony of the "recognition procession" by having Tom reject his mother when she reaches for him out of the crowd: "I do not know you, woman"—this is for Leslie Fiedler the "unforgivable sin" (270) and the most quintessentially American moment in the novel—harsher, it would seem, than Winnicott's loss, forgetfulness, and sadness.

Lacan sees the ego as forever incomplete, illusory, and desiring; his reformulation of Freud is not comforting, but does acknowledge the depth of our fascination with that Other who looks like us; he reminds us of our sense that our ego, no matter how well shored up, is still fragile and can still merge, for good or ill, with the Other. Narcissus gazing into his own reflection is the mythic embodiment of this desire, the personification of blurred ego boundaries; Plato imagined that we all seek the other half of ourselves.

Certainly Twain was far from unique in his fascination with twinship and doubling. Poe, Andersen, Wilde, Maupassant, and E.T.A. Hoffmann offer chilling tales of doubling; the shadow-self motif permeates the beliefs of many pre-verbal cultures especially in the dread of mirrors and portraits; Victor Turner has eloquently described the twinship rituals among the Ndembu in which they acknowledge this freak of nature as, in Turner's words, mystery and absurdity, "a huge and even brutal joke" (85).

While *twin* is the term used for the biological phenomenon, *imposter* the legal term, and *double* or *shadow* the words we use in the imaginative or spiritual realm, it is difficult to tease them apart in the imagination. Each term calls up the other psychologically, and is embedded in our notions of the Other. The ubiquity of the fascination with twins and doubling in literature and in life, and the collapse of rational explanation in the face of the phenomenon, certainly suggests the presence of some basic desire: for double strength, for the ability to trick others, for invulnerability and immortality, but most of all, I suggest, for a sense of completeness.

Jules Glenn and others have studied twins psychoanalytically. Twins, they find, have difficulty resolving their oedipal conflicts; they may have a tendency to cheat and steal, growing from the sense that some part of themselves has been stolen from them. They may unconsciously deal with others as if the others were twins as well; they seem to see a world "filled with twins," and in this way dilute their feelings toward their real twin. Their most characteristic defenses are projection and identification, defenses which grow from confusion of self and object. They may deliberately choose different fields of endeavor, sensing that in doing so they will make one complete person. They find the chief rewards of twinship to be the enhancement of empathy and of creativity.

In all of this, one theme emerges: the blurring of ego boundaries, a notion in most psychoanalytic theory that suggests poor ego development. But literature and experience suggest that we singletons envy twins, and consciously or unconsciously search for a twin of our own. We lack, and we desire, even in its illusory form, those blurred boundaries, that empathy, that creativity, that sense of completion. Lacan's language is negative—the illusory, even paranoid ego, the ego as "alienating identity"—but his recognition of the ubiquity of desire, of unstable ego, offers a way of understanding the essential human fascination with twins.

Since its first appearance in print, critics have praised the plot of *The Prince and The Pauper* for symmetry, logic, completeness—unlike the plot of anything else Twain wrote. The majority of twentieth-century critics, though, have claimed that Twain's wife Olivia, and his genteel Nook Farm friends and neighbors, who loved the book, exerted an emasculating influence on his composition of it, feminizing Twain's natural—i.e. masculine—enjoyment of rough edges, crude humor, and literary disorder. For these critics, that very symmetry marks it as a children's book, something too simple and obvious for adult tastes.

I wonder whether that symmetry, that balance—which is in fact a characteristic of much children's literature—may represent, at some deep level, the mother's face, smiling at us, giving us back ourselves, allowing our narcissistic child selves to surface, to anticipate, to enjoy, to feel confident. For Winnicott, a return to such blurred ego boundaries is occasionally restful, but it may also awaken the restless fears of ego dissolution, of merging, of losing one's identity. For Lacan, we live always in such a state of longing, for both completion and for separation.

Works Cited

Baetzhold, Howard. *Mark Twain and John Bull*. Bloomington: Indiana University Press, 1970.

Benvenuto, Bice, and Roger Kennedy. *The Works of Jacques Lacan*. New York: St. Martin's, 1986.

Fiedler, Leslie. *Love and Death in the American Novel*. New York: Stein, 1966.

Glenn, Jules. "Twins in the Theatre: A Study of Plays by Peter and Anthony Shaffer." In *Blood Brothers*. Ed. Norman Kiell. 277–299. New York: International University Press, 1983.

Lacan, Jacques. "The Mirror Stages." In *Ecrits: A Selection*. Trans. Alan Sheridan. 1–7. New York: Norton, 1977.

Rank, Otto. *The Double*. Chapel Hill: University of North Carolina Press, 1971.

Turner, Victor. *The Ritual Process*. Ithaca: Cornell University Press, 1969.

Twain, Mark. *The Prince and the Pauper*. Eds. Fischer and Salamo. Berkeley: University of California Press, 1979.

Winnicott, D. W. "Communication Between Infants and Mothers." In *Babies and Their Mothers*. 89–103. Reading, MA: Addison Wesley, 1988.
_____. "Mirror Role of Mother and Family." In *Playing and Reality*. 111–118. London: Routledge, 1971.

CHAPTER 8

Childhood Fantasies and Frustrations in Maurice Sendak's Picture Books

Lucy Rollin

> What really shapes and conditions and makes us is somebody only
> a few of us ever have the courage to face: and that is the child you
> once were, long before formal education ever got its claws into
> you—that impatient, all-demanding child who wants love and
> power and can't get enough of either and who goes on raging and
> weeping in your spirit till at last your eyes are closed and all the fools
> say "Doesn't he look peaceful?" It is those pent-up, craving children
> who make all the wars and all the horrors and all the art and all the
> beauty and discovery in life, because they are trying to achieve what
> lay beyond their grasp before they were five years old.
>
> —Robertson Davies, *The Rebel Angels*

The creature Freud called the paragon of all the vices breaks through occasionally in adult literature (*Lolita*, *Lord of the Flies*), but almost never do
we see the raging, craving inner child in the books we give our children—
so deep is our need to protect ourselves from that image. The work of Maurice Sendak is the one exception in children's literature. His books depict
the Freudian child more completely, more forthrightly, and more sympa-
thetically than those of any other children's writer. This essay focuses on his
most famous—and for many adults, most disturbing—books: *Where the Wild
Things Are* (1963), *In the Night Kitchen* (1970), and *Outside Over There* (1981).

These three picture books, which Sendak has labeled a trilogy, are the province of the deepest Freudian themes in his work. Although designed and written over a period of twenty years, they have a single motif: how children learn to control their feelings. Each plot describes a child experiencing some frustration, entering a fantasy world, projecting and controlling powerful feelings, and returning to the everyday world calmed and coping. Freud called the acquisition of such control the child's "greatest cultural achievement" (*Beyond* 15). Moreover, Sendak shares Freud's commitment to the value of the fantasy life; his protagonists find in their fantasies the tools which allow them to live at peace in the world. Such fantasies are far from play; they are in fact the most serious work.

The three books have basically the same format: few words to a page, sequential pictures, and a movement from smaller to larger and back to smaller pictures. The largest pictures are in the center of each book, in the center of each protagonist's fantasy; the rhythmic swelling and receding of the illustrations are matched in all three by the rhythmic, almost incantatory texts. The differences between the books are equally significant. The first book describes young Max, the second a slightly older Mickey, and the third an older child still—a female: Ida. In addition, Ida has a younger sister, while Max and Mickey have no siblings in evidence. Thus the book offers a kind of analogue to a child's growth: from younger to older, from anal to genital, and—inevitably, in the Freudian sense—from comic to tragic.

The element in *Where the Wild Things Are* which most disturbed adults when the book appeared in 1963 was its assumption of hostility and aggression in a normal child. Like Little Hans, Max is a "paragon of all the vices" (*Sexual Enlightenment* 57). He wears his wolf suit complete with large claws, and drives nails into the wall to make himself a tent; he hangs his stuffed animal from a coat hanger and chases the family dog with a fork. His mischief culminates in his yelling at his mother, "I'll eat you up!" Max is a child in Freud's second pregenital phase: sadistic-anal, in which the desire for mastery is the greatest component. Max wants to master everything in his environment, greedily and violently. His behavior is hardly unfamiliar to mothers of normal children. These mothers must invariably exert the parental authority that Max's mother does: she sends him to his room without his supper.

In Max's fantasy, he vents and conquers his aggression toward his mother by creating "wild things" much bigger and more powerful than he: creatures who "roared their terrible roars and gnashed their terrible teeth and rolled their terrible eyes and showed their terrible claws." No mother likes to see herself in such a vengeful guise, although many children occasionally see their mothers so. But these creatures are also projections of Max's own aggression, feelings bigger than he is.

Sendak's drawings of these creatures also disturbed adults when the book appeared. Amalgams of various animals, with incongruous horns, hair, claws, scales, sharp teeth, and webbed feet, they occupy great space in the pictures, in contrast to small Max. But Sendak carefully prepared the reader to recognize these creatures as products of Max himself: in the second illustration of the book, a drawing of a similar creature is tacked up on the wall, with the inscription, "by Max." Similarly, Little Hans' fears of a giraffe became more understandable when Freud and Hans' father remembered that Hans had a picture of a giraffe over his bed (*Sexual Enlightenment* 79).

One wild thing is especially interesting. As Max tames the wild things he first meets, one creature peers from the undergrowth at the far right of the picture. In the next picture, it emerges to join the group. It has human feet, the only wild thing which does, and is the most openly masculine, in its resemblance to a bull. In the second wild rumpus picture at the center of the book, he is the only creature facing completely away from Max, and in the third wild rumpus picture, Max is astride this creature, who looks in fact more menacing than ever.

It is tempting to speculate that this might be a projection of Max's father, as well as of Max's own aggression. Freud reminds us that every daydream is motivated by an erotic wish, and he mentions the "sexually exciting effect of many emotions which in themselves are unpleasurable, such as feelings of apprehension, fright, or horror" (*Interpretation* 69). The horrific nature of these wild things supplies Max—and the children who identify with him as they read—this titillation, as well as the need for activity and mastery.

This is the key notion in the book: mastery. Max has conquered these wild things "with the magic trick of staring into all their yellow eyes without blinking once." Max is in power, having projected and then conquered his own aggression. This book also illustrates the compulsion to repeat a frightening situation, in this case Max's mother's threat and superior power, and the implied power of his father, by becoming active rather than remaining passive: "As the child passes over from the passivity of the experience to the activity of the game, he hands on the disagreeable experience ... and in this way revenges himself on a substitute" (*Beyond* 17). That Max's substitutes are fantasy creatures in no way minimizes their effectiveness; as Freud says, psychic reality is what counts.

Freud himself, in *The Interpretation of Dreams*, described a child who was sent to bed without supper and then dreamed of a huge feast, not incidentally a feast of meat. The boy wished for such a feast, and the dream fulfilled his wish; but in this dream, the boy himself did not eat the feast. "Education had already begun to have an effect on him," says Freud, and produced the early dream distortion (*Interpretation* 302). In Max's daydream, however, Max himself gets his feast of aggression and hostility, as well as his real dinner. The ending therefore is comic, in the Shakespearean sense: tensions resolved, order established, satisfaction all around.

In the Night Kitchen is also comic on a superficial level as well as on a dramatic and philosophic one. When it appeared in 1970, elite critics of children's literature were surprised, and some even offended, by its frankly comic-book format. The flatness of the pictures, their vivid colors and bold shapes, the openly commercial reference to brand names, the Oliver Hardy bakers, and the "balloons" containing the text—all this suggested to some that Sendak had abandoned "serious" literature for children. But like *Where the Wild Things Are, In the Night Kitchen* is serious in the Freudian sense, as distinguished from what is real (*Critical Theory* 749).

The fantasy of *In the Night Kitchen* is sensual rather than aggressive; this is a book full of infantile sexuality in all the manifestations Freud described. It begins with a "racket in the night," thumps and bumps coming from the parents' room which children recognize, unconsciously, as caused by some activity of their parents they are forbidden to see. For Freud, this scopophilia, as he called it, is quite normal, even arousing. Mickey calls out, "Quiet down there!"—an exhortation which might be directed at his own genitals as well as the noises.

Then he falls "out of his clothes, past the moon, past his mama and papa sleeping tight," into the Night Kitchen, a place of adult activity. Here that activity is making cake, an empirical fact (bakers really do bake at night) which merges with Mickey's fantasy, just as the day's residues merge with our latent desires and form our dreams (*Interpretation* 594–603).

In this kitchen, Mickey experiences great sensual pleasure: he finds himself in bread dough; he "kneaded and punched it and pounded and pulled"; he flies "up and up and up"; he dives into milk, swims, pours, sings, crows, and slides easily back into his bed, happy and relaxed. He revels, Freud might say, in his polymorphous perversity; for, if Max represents the sadistic-anal phase of infantile sexuality, Mickey represents a later phase which Freud called the second phase of infantile masturbation, which appears usually before the fourth year.

Masturbation, says Freud, represents the "executive agency of the whole of infantile sexuality" (*Three Essays* 55), and certainly Mickey seems happy to activate that agency. Some critics have been uncomfortable with this interpretation of the book and have suggested a bed wetting fantasy instead. But Freud confounds these critics. For manifestation of sexuality at this stage, he says, is most often displayed by the "urinary apparatus … on behalf of the still undeveloped sexual apparatus" (*Three Essays* 56). Thus bed wetting corresponds to a nocturnal emission. Mickey's sexuality is truly polymorphous, as is, Freud reminds us several times, that of most children.

The pictures in this book are richer than those in *Where the Wild Things Are*. They are packed with details, most of them concerned with food: cake, jam, salt, baking soda, flour, tomatoes, coconut, oats, asparagus, berries, cream, and of course, milk. There is an array of utensils, too: egg beaters, mixing cups, salt boxes, shakers, corkscrews, grinders, nutcrackers. There is further interesting detail as Mickey begins his flight in his bread dough airplane: he flies past two containers of baby food, and a box of oats labeled "first, cheapest, best." Then he flies up over the words "delicious treat" and "special" and "wonder" until, on the large, luminous double-page spread that marks the center of the book and the center of Mickey's fantasy, he is poised over a large milk bottle, the three bakers small below, all the kitchen utensils and food arrayed behind him, and the picture of a baby to the far right. It is difficult not to read this as Mickey's unconscious understanding that the thumps and bumps he hears in the night from his parents' room have to do with making babies, with milky liquid, and with his own pleasurable physical activity.

The text contains an interesting reversal which links Mickey's masturbatory activity, the idea of making babies, and the kitchen setting. Upon Mickey's arrival in the Night Kitchen, the bakers mistake him for milk and mix him in batter, putting him in the "Mickey oven" to bake a "delicious Mickey cake." It is only a short step from this depiction to the folk saying that an unborn child is something "in the oven." Then Mickey pokes through, in a birth analogue, saying "I'm not the milk and the milk's not me. I'm Mickey!" He has achieved his own identity. But when he provides milk for the bakers, he sings, "I'm in the milk and the milk's in me. God bless milk and God bless me!" This little rhyme sums up the paradox of human procreation: we are truly "in the milk" as seminal human beings, and the "milk" is in us as well, first in the male and then in the female, to create new, separate, complete individuals like Mickey.

Mickey's joyful blessings affirm his participation in that paradoxical process which links him with the adult society of the bakers and their activity, against the "cityscape" of the food and utensils. Certainly for Freud, as well as for the rest of us, making babies and participating in—or making—society are intricately related, psychologically as well as physically.

I am not suggesting that children—or even parents or many literary critics—consciously perceive this level of meaning in *In the Night Kitchen*, though it is surely there. Perhaps if adults had, in fact, the book would not have suffered the vilification and even suppression, in some quarters, that it has. For if *Where the Wild Things Are* marked the first honest depiction of aggression in a normal child, *In the Night Kitchen* marked the first depiction of full frontal nudity in a male child in a book designed for the young. Parents and librarians hastened to protect children from the pictures, some even drawing tempera diapers on Mickey. But of course, what most adults were really resisting was the rich sensual pleasure so fully depicted in the book. Mickey represents that pleasure in one's own body that we all experience as children: no fear of mess or liquids or our own genitals or excrement, and even a pleasurable association of all this with food and human society.

Our infantile amnesia, as Freud called it, causes us to conceal from ourselves the beginning of our sexual lives, our early polymorphous perversity. But the children who found this book a joyful celebration have been, so far, untouched by that amnesia and have responded to it at its deepest level: as a gloriously comic book in every sense—stylistically, thematically, even cosmically.

In the third book of the trilogy, *Outside Over There*, the protagonist is a girl; she is somewhat older than Max and Mickey, and she has a baby sister. Here is the heart of the plot and of the tragic undertone which marks this story, in contrast to the comic resolutions of the other two books. And while *Where the Wild Things Are* and *In the Night Kitchen* are hardly exhausted by these discussions, no description of *Outside Over There* can hope to tap the complexities in it, for it must surely be one of the richest picture books ever designed for children.

The plot is relatively simple: Ida "played her wonder horn to rock the baby still—but never watched.—So the goblins came." These "goblins" steal away her baby sister, leaving an "ice thing" in its place. Ida goes to the world of Outside Over There where she rescues her baby sister from the goblins. Then she returns with the baby to her mother—on the surface, a happy ending. But the pictures belie that happiness, adding a depth and wealth of Freudian reverberations. I will examine here only two of them, but they are important ones and clearly interwoven: hostility toward siblings and the female oedipal complex.

The very beginning of the book is marked by menace: a hooded figure follows Ida, who is loaded down with her baby sister, even on the dedication page; two hooded figures appear on the first page; and on the second page, Ida struggles with the crying baby while her mother simply gazes out to sea and the hooded figures creep away with a ladder. All of this foreboding is established only visually; thus the reader is prepared for the text when it says that Ida never watched the baby. The pictures have already let us see Ida's unconscious hostility.

Freud reflected on the "disunity" between siblings: "Children love themselves first, and it is only later that they learn to love others.... There is no doubt that the small child hates his siblings as his competitors" (*Introductory Lectures* 204). Many of us harbor evil wishes against our siblings well into adulthood, Freud noted; wishes which often appear in dreams. All of this is quite normal and, in itself, no surprise to parents. What may surprise parents is the power of these feelings: "We rarely form a correct idea of the strength of these jealous impulses, of the tenacity with which they persist.... A powerful tendency to aggressiveness is always present beside a powerful love..." (*New Introductory Lectures* 123–4).

The ensuing pictures in *Outside Over There* show Ida's rage and hostility. The sunflowers, which at first only peeped in the window, now proliferate and intrude, no longer peaceful. The landscape outside another window shows the onset of a violent storm. On the surface, the hostile flowers and the storm reflect Ida's anger that the baby has been stolen by the goblins. But the menace was already present, so Ida's rage must spring from a deeper source: that of having a sibling at all, and the significance of that event for Ida's relationship with her parents.

For most children, as Freud said, hate their siblings even to the point of wishing them dead. "To children," he commented, "being dead means approximately the same thing as being 'gone.' Thus if a child has reasons for wishing the absence of another, there is nothing to restrain him from giving his wish the form of the other child being dead" (*Interpretation* 288–9). Ida has perhaps unconsciously wished her sister dead; part of the anger she feels may spring from this guilty wish, as well as from her displacement from her parents. And to those who would argue that Sendak's pictures overstate Ida's violent feelings, Freud had an answer: "Analysis of children's play has shown ... that the aggressive impulses of little girls leave nothing to be desired in the way of abundance and violence" (*New Introductory Lectures* 118).

Much has been written about Freud's bewilderment over the female; certainly he admitted that bewilderment on more than one occasion.

Nevertheless his struggles to formulate the female oedipal complex reveal a deep sympathy toward women and certainly a desire to understand them, and his tragic view of life comes to the fore much more often in these discussions than in his discussions of the male oedipal complex. For Freud, the "circuitous path" that a girl must travel to both enter and resolve her complex often reaches no particular end; in the girl, Freud believed, the whole process was frequently doomed to failure. Sendak's book, while ending happily on the surface, really demonstrates this failure.

Ida's father, throughout the book, is "away at sea," and her mother sits in the arbor lost in her own thoughts while Ida tends the baby. When Ida discovers that the baby is missing, her words are "They stole my sister away—to be a nasty goblin's bride!" Why would Ida think in terms of being a bride, unless she herself would like to be one? Yet her father, so far away, cannot satisfy her oedipal desire for him. Ida wears her mother's cloak, much too big for her, to the world of Outside Over There where she finds herself "Smack in the middle of a wedding." Like Mickey in *In the Night Kitchen*, Ida seems to have discovered how babies are made, for in this fantasy world, babies are everywhere, all looking exactly like Ida's sister.

What Ida has experienced here, and fled into fantasy to learn to cope with, is the crisis in her oedipal complex. To Freud, all children are innately bisexual and experience very early strong desire for both the mother and the father; in his later writing he posited the special strength of the mother attachment in girls, which made the love for the father all the more ambivalent (*New Introductory Lectures* 119–20).

In girls, too, Freud noted that the castration complex is not a threat, but an accomplished fact: the girl has no penis. It is this discovery, Freud believes, which causes the girl to settle on her identification with her mother, at the same time repressing her anger at learning that both she and her mother are damaged. She then takes the father as a love-object; this is the oedipal complex in its feminine form, when the "most powerful feminine wish" is for a baby by the father (*New Introductory Lectures* 128).

The repressed love and desire for the mother remain as well, however, maintaining the ambivalence in these wishes. And after the girl's oedipal complex is established, her mother inevitably becomes an authority who restricts the girl's sexuality, "imposing on her the renunciation of sexual freedom which society demands" (*Introductory Lectures* 205). Sendak suggests this in his pictures, for Ida's mother seems to ignore her struggles with the heavy baby, a note of pathos which is only visual and does not appear in the text.

The proliferation of babies in Ida's fantasy suggests an overwhelming knowledge which has come to her: her mother is her father's love object, the one by whom he has babies. Ida can never be such an object for her father. Those babies therefore are goblins, in the shape of her baby sister. But Ida does not remain passive. In her fantasy, like Max and Mickey, she becomes active.

Freud commented that "the swing-over from passivity to activity does not take place with the same regularity and vigor in all children," but that he could predict in it the relative strength of the masculine and feminine identifications which would be revealed in adult sexual life (*Sexuality* 205). Ida's aggressive horn-blowing, even though it is in her fantasy, suggests that she will maintain some of her masculine tendencies. For now, however, in the real world she acquiesces in the renunciation of her instinctual desire for her father and takes up her feminine duties. She picks up the baby sister and moves slowly along a "stream that curled like a path" back to her mother.

Freud's sympathy for such a girl's plight was eloquently expressed: "What occasions the decay [of the oedipal complex in girls]? The little girl who wants to believe herself her father's beloved and partner in love must one day endure a harsh punishment at his hands, and finds herself hurled to earth from the cloud-castles" (*Passing* 176). In her disappointment she must take her "younger sister as a substitute for the baby she has vainly wished for from her father" (*Introductory Lectures* 334).

Sendak's pictures are equally eloquent. As Ida finds her "real" baby sister in an eggshell, her face is ambiguous, neither smiling nor sad, and her gesture does not quite reach for the baby. She goes away from her fantasy world through a strange landscape which appears peaceful and beautiful, but as she moves toward the right of the picture, a menacing tree and a dark space await her, and as she meets her mother, the large dog adds a note of portent. Sendak's text as the book ends is also equivocal: a letter from her father reads, "I'll be home one day, and my brave bright little Ida must watch the baby and her Mama for her Papa, who loves her always." This seems a rather large order for a child who is still struggling with her ambivalent feelings. The final text reads, "Which is just what Ida did."—a sentence which on the surface seems to bring the book to a happy ending. But what Ida must do, really, is put aside her hopes and desires and face the harsh reality that her father is forever unavailable to her and that she must content herself with substitutes.

The final picture shows Ida, again with an expressionless face, supporting the baby as it takes a step. The sunflowers which earlier marked Ida's swelling rage are now tamed behind a small fence, some even covering their "faces" in a gesture of equivocation which once again matches Ida's state: she knows, now, but she may not see.

If discomfort marked the critical reception of *Where the Wild Things Are*, and dismay and anger that of *In the Night Kitchen*, consternation is the best way to describe the critical reception which attended the publication of *Outside Over There*. It was reviewed as "quite simply magnificent" and "drearily nostalgic and sentimental." Enlightened parents who know they should buy Sendak found themselves bewildered by the book. It was distributed in both adult and children's markets (a move which delighted Sendak) by the publisher, Harper and Row. Such confusion, although it distresses parents and critics who like their children's books in neat categories, is a tribute to the book itself. For, like Freud, Sendak is suggesting that living is a difficult and unfinished business, and that compromise is what is ultimately required of all of us. "All knowledge is patchwork, and each step forward leaves an unsolved residue behind" (*Sexual Enlightenment* 138).

These three picture books, then, taken together, offer an image of the child that Freud believed was in all of us: curious, sexual, hostile, aggressive, loving and desiring, struggling to control powerful instincts, finding aid in an active fantasy life. It is not an image that most adults like to look at; hence the dubious critical and parental reception of Sendak's work. Children have not shrunk from this image, though, recognizing themselves—and Sendak's sympathy for them—with clear-eyed fortitude. The most famous story about Sendak's effect on the young has circulated for years. An autistic girl who had never spoken said her first sentence after an adult read *Where the Wild Things Are* with her. It was, "Can I have that book?"

Works Cited

Freud, Sigmund. *The Interpretation of Dreams* (1900). New York: Avon Books, 1965.
_____. *Three Essays on the Theory of Sexuality* (1905). New York: Basic Books, 1962.
_____. "The Sexual Enlightenment of Children," "Family Romances," "Analysis of Phobia in a Five-Year-Old Boy." In *The Sexual Enlightenment of Children*. Ed. Philip Rieff. New York: Collier Books, 1963.
_____. "Creative Writers and Daydreaming." In *Critical Theory Since Plato*. Ed. Hazard Adams. New York: Harcourt Brace Jovanovich, 1971.
_____. *Introductory Lectures on Psychoanalysis* (1917). New York: Norton, 1966.
_____. *Beyond the Pleasure Principle* (1920). In vol. 18 of *The Standard Edition of the Complete Psychological Works of Sigmund Freud*. Trans. James Strachey. 24 vols. London: Hogarth Press, 1955.

_____. *The Ego and the Id* (1923). New York: Norton, 1962.

_____. "The Passing of the Oedipus Complex," "Some Psychological Consequences of the Anatomical Distinction Between the Sexes," "Female Sexuality." In *Sexuality and the Psychology of Love*. Ed. Philip Rieff. New York: Collier Books, 1963.

_____. *New Introductory Lectures on Psychoanalysis*. 1932. New York: Norton, 1965.

Sendak, Maurice. *Where the Wild Things Are*. New York: Harper and Row, 1963.

_____. *In the Night Kitchen*. New York: Harper and Row, 1970.

_____. *Outside Over There*. New York: Harper and Row, 1981.

CHAPTER 9

The Grotesque and the Taboo in Roald Dahl's Humorous Writings for Children

Mark I. West

When Jacob, one of my godsons, had his fourth birthday, I gave him a copy of Roald Dahl's *The Twits*. I usually mail him his present because we live in different states, but this time I gave it to him in person. The morning after his birthday, Jacob asked me to read the book to him. I agreed, and after breakfast Jacob, his mother, and I went into the living room where I began reading.

The story begins with a humorous tirade against beards, especially Mr. Twit's beard. At the end of this tirade, Dahl describes some of the food particles caught in Mr. Twit's whiskers. "If you peered deep into the moustachy bristles sticking out over his upper lip," Dahl writes, "you would probably see ... things that had been there for months and months, like a piece of maggoty green cheese or a moldy old cornflake or even the slimy tail of a tinned sardine" (7).

Upon hearing this passage, Jacob's mother groaned, pronounced the book disgusting, and left the room. Jacob and I, however, were laughing so hard that we hardly noticed her departure. We spent the next several minutes searching through my beard and pretending to find all sorts of revolting things.

This incident came to mind while I was reading David Rees' attack on Dahl in the fall 1988 issue of *Children's Literature in Education*. Rees condemns nearly all of Dahl's children's books, but he singles out *The Twits* as one of the worst. According to Rees, the book teaches children that "bearded people are dirty and are trying to hide their real appearance" (146). He goes on to say that the book leads children "to think that all ugly people are evil" (147). Adult readers, Rees argues, would not take Dahl's statements about beards seriously, but he maintains that young children probably would. In recalling Jacob's reaction to *The Twits*, I cannot help but question Rees' line of reasoning. Jacob certainly did not take Dahl's attack on beards seriously, and I never got the impression that he thought of me as evil because I have a beard.

As I see it, the person who may be taking the book too seriously is Rees, but his reaction is not especially surprising. Adults often deplore as tasteless many of the stories, situations, and jokes that children find humorous. This conflict, however, involves more than taste; it also involves differences in the psychology of children and adults. These differences help explain why Dahl's books are so popular with children and so disliked by Rees and other similarly minded adults.

An aspect of *The Twits* that appeals more strongly to children than to adults is the disgusting nature of Mr. and Mrs. Twit. These horrid people not only look disgusting, but they do some pretty disgusting things to each other. On one occasion, Mrs. Twit puts her glass eye in Mr. Twit's beer mug, and he nearly swallows it. Another time she pours spaghetti sauce over a plateful of live worms and serves it to her unsuspecting husband. Mr. Twit is just as bad. He, for example, sticks a slimy frog in Mrs. Twit's bed and then fools her into thinking that the frog is a deadly monster. The gross pranks that the Twits play on each other generally seem funny to children, but to Rees such pranks are truly revolting.

In an attempt to explain why children often laugh at that which adults may find disgusting, Paul E. McGhee, a child psychologist and author of *Humor: Its Origin and Development*, finds it helpful to examine the psychological dynamics associated with toilet training. As he points out, the idea that certain things or actions are disgusting is usually absorbed while children are experiencing bladder and bowel training. "Parents," he writes, "seem to be very concerned about just when and where these acts occur, and become very upset when they occur at the wrong place or the wrong time. Even the most easy-going parents may be embarrassed or angered at untimely messes" (80). Such parental responses usually spark feelings of anxiety in children, and one way that they deal with their anxiety is through humor.

For very young children, this form of humor is expressed without a hint of subtlety. McGhee gives the example of a three-year-old who finds it hilarious to "approach another child or an adult and say 'poop' or 'kaka'" (130). Although school-age children still experience anxieties related to the pressures of measuring up to adult standards of cleanliness and neatness, they no longer find the utterance of words such as "poop" quite so funny. McGhee expands on this point in his book:

> It becomes boring simply to say taboo words, so more complicated and interesting ways of expressing "toiletness" are created. This pattern continues throughout the child's development; that is, new ways of joking about the sources of tension are developed as new intellectual capacities evolve. The underlying conflict may be the same, but children generally prefer intellectually challenging ways of joking about conflicts [80].

Much of the humor in *The Twits* is very similar to the jokes that children make about cleanliness, bodily functions, and other related topics. It has scatological connotations, but there is still a facade of respectability. Thus, when Dahl calls Mr. Twit "a foul and smelly old man" (7) or describes the worm spaghetti as "too squishy" (16), he strikes a chord with many children.

The humor that runs through Dahl's depictions of revolting behavior is enhanced, at least in the opinions of children, by the fact that he often attributes such behavior to adults. Psychologists have long noted that children enjoy jokes and stories that poke fun at the moral authority of adults. In Martha Wolfenstein's seminal study entitled *Children's Humor: A Psychological Analysis*, published in 1954, she points out that this aspect of children's humor is tied to the unequal power relationship between children and adults:

> Children find ways of making fun of the bigness, power, and prerogatives of the grown-ups whom they envy. There is another imposing aspect of adults, which is often oppressive and fearful to children, namely their moral authority; and here, too, children seek relief through mockery. They seize with delight on opportunities to show that the grown-ups are not infallibly good [45].

In creating Mr. and Mrs. Twit, Dahl provides children with two prime examples of adult characters who are by no means infallibly good. Another Dahl character who plays this role is the grandmother in *George's Marvelous Medicine*, the book Rees denounces as "the most repellent of all Roald Dahl's books for the young" (148). Like Mr. and Mrs. Twit, Grandma, as she is called, is physically repulsive. Dahl describes her as having "pale brown teeth and a small puckered-up mouth like a dog's bottom" (2). Her behavior, however, is worse than her looks. As Dahl puts it, "she was always complaining, grousing, grouching, grumbling, griping about something or other.... She didn't seem to care about other people, only herself. She was a miserable old grouch" (2). Grandma is especially mean to her grandson, George, always ordering him about, criticizing his every move, and trying to make him eat various insects. Dahl clearly intends for Grandma to function as a comical character, but this only partially explains why children find the book funny.

Much of the humor in *George's Marvelous Medicine* relates to George's decision to get even with Grandma. He creates a ghastly concoction of cleaning products, foodstuffs, automobile fluids, and practically everything else that he finds around the house and pours a little bit of it into the jar containing Grandma's medicine. When Grandma takes a spoonful of George's brew, she undergoes a whole array of ridiculous transformations before finally coming to an amazing end. As even this brief plot summary shows, George's aggression plays a major role in the story, but it is dealt with in such a humorous and whimsical manner that children often find it hilarious.

By using humor and fantasy to mitigate the aggressive elements of the story, Dahl employs essentially the same technique that children learn to use when expressing feelings of hostility. This technique was described by Sigmund Freud in *Jokes and Their Relation to the Unconscious*:

> Though as children we are still endowed with a powerful inherited disposition to hostility, we are later taught ... to renounce the expression of hostility by deeds.... A joke will allow us to exploit something ridiculous in our enemy which we could not ... bring forward openly or consciously.... The joke will evade restrictions and open sources of pleasure that have become inaccessible [102–103].

Like the jokes that Freud mentions, *George's Marvelous Medicine* and many of Dahl's other books provide children with forms of pleasure that cannot be found in many other children's books. He succeeds in doing this not just by using the same kinds of humor that children use themselves, but also by sympathizing with children in their conflicts with adults. During a recent interview, Dahl discussed this point, and in the process he came close to echoing Freud's position:

> I generally write for children between the ages of seven and nine. At these ages, children are only semicivilized. They are in the

process of becoming civilized, and the people who are doing the civ-
ilizing are the adults around them, specifically their parents and
their teachers. Because of this, children are inclined, at least sub-
consciously, to regard grown-ups as the enemy. I see this as natural,
and I often work it into my children's books. That's why the grown-
ups in my books are sometimes silly or grotesque. I like to poke fun
at grown-ups, especially the pretentious ones and the grouchy ones
[Qtd. in West 74–75].

There can be little doubt that children enjoy the way in which Dahl
treats his grouchy old characters. He is, after all, one of the best-selling
children's authors of our time. However, some adults, including Rees, feel
that Dahl mistreats his adult characters. Rees is especially upset at the fate
of George's grandmother. He argues that Dahl is teaching children that
grumpy people "deserve to be poisoned and killed" (149).

This interpretation, of course, is based on a literal reading of the book
and, according to a recent study, is one that most children do not share.
When Charles Gerard Van Renen surveyed a group of school children about
their reactions to *George's Marvelous Medicine*, he found that "few respon-
dents were prepared to take the situation seriously"; they felt "that the
events of this fantasy would find no ready transfer to real life" (19).

Perhaps the reason Rees interprets Dahl's books so literally and seriously is that he cannot appreciate the humor in them. It is often difficult
for adults to see anything funny about children's jokes, and the same probably applies to books that are intended to appeal to the less civilized side
of children's sense of humor. As Martha Wolfenstein points out, this is
"because the adult and the child rarely find themselves in the same emotional situation at the same time" (214). Wolfenstein, however, holds out
hope for the Reeses of the world. She argues that the key to appreciating
the humor of children is to put ourselves in their place. "Children," she
writes, "are not so remote from us. If we cannot always laugh with them,
we can at times laugh like them" (214).

Works Cited

Dahl, Roald. *George's Marvelous Medicine*. London: Cape, 1981.
_____. *The Twits*. London: Cape, 1980.
Freud, Sigmund. *Jokes and Their Relation to the Unconscious*. In vol. 8 of *The Standard
    Edition of the Complete Psychological Works of Sigmund Freud*. Trans. James Strachey.
    24 vols. London: Hogarth, 1960.
McGhee, Paul E. *Humor: Its Origin and Development*. San Francisco: W. H. Freeman,
    1979.

Rees, David. "Dahl's Chickens: Roald Dahl." In *Children's Literature in Education*, 19 (1988): 143–155.

Van Renen, Charles Gerard. *A Critical Review of Some of Roald Dahl's Books for Children, with Particular Reference to a "Subversive" Element in His Writing*. Master's thesis, Rhodes University, 1985.

West, Mark I. *Trust Your Children: Voices Against Censorship in Children's Literature*, New York: Neal-Schuman, 1988.

Wolfenstein, Martha. *Children's Humor: A Psychological Analysis*. Bloomington: Indiana University Press, 1978.

CHAPTER 10

Good-Enough
Mother Hubbard

Lucy Rollin

As I write this, it is Mother's Day, ending another month-long public out-pouring of sentimental affection and gratitude—on billboards, church and department store marquees, restaurant windows, florists' signs, and end-less greeting card counters—to the Good Mother. Once again I have won-dered, in my psychoanalytic way, how much these professions of love compensate for guilty feelings of resentment and anger. Some of the moth-ers I saw at brunch today, surrounded by children and grandchildren who were trying too hard, seemed slightly grumpy, as if they were tolerating the attention but really knew what lay at the heart of it.

Our culture doesn't allow much overlap between good and bad when it comes to mothers. The history of Mother's Day is proof. When it was first proposed in 1858, Anna Reeves Jarvis meant it to encourage women to work together for better sanitation, and then to become politically active for peace between the warring sides as the Civil War ended (Coontz 152). In Boston in 1872, Julia Ward Howe proposed a Mothers' Day for women opposed to war. By 1905 Anna Jarvis, daughter of Anna Reeves Jarvis, again campaigned for a Mothers' Day to encourage women to be politi-cally active, but she ran head-on into opposition from those who insisted mothers should remain at home, attentive to their families. Merchants who foresaw a money-making opportunity especially opposed Jarvis' concept.

When Congress finally adopted a Mother's Day in 1914, it had changed from a celebration of plural *mothers*, acting in the public sphere for peace and cooperation, to a celebration of singular *mother*, at home: "The history of Mother's Day is a microcosm of the simultaneous sentimentalization and commercialization of private life" (Coontz 153). "Good mother" is where she belongs, home alone; "bad mother" is out making trouble with other people.

Analyst and pediatrician D. W. Winnicott created the concept of the "good-enough" mother in an attempt to provide a middle ground: a mother who loves and hates her baby at once, in a true ambivalence, and who finds ways—consciously and unconsciously—to acknowledge both feelings.[1] One way, he commented, is through nursery rhymes, which often express violent feelings toward children. He imagined her singing "Rockabye Baby, on the tree top": "This is not a sentimental rhyme. Sentimentality is useless for parents, as it contains a denial of hate, and sentimentality in a mother is no good at all from the infant's point of view"; then the infant cannot learn to tolerate its own feelings of hate ("Hate in the Countertransference" 202). For a baby, too, is ambivalent, hating its mother because she cannot always satisfy all its needs, and loving her with an intensity and dependency we adults can barely imagine.

Winnicott does not mention "Old Mother Hubbard," one of the most popular of all the nursery rhymes, yet it is, in my view, an almost perfect representation of the ambivalence of both mother and child. And since the rhymes are kept alive by parents first, repeating them to their children, and then by the children themselves, this rhyme's simultaneous address to parent and child accounts, I believe, for that enormous popularity. In this essay, I explore the history of the rhyme and interpret it from the standpoint of the child and then of the mother, using Winnicott's theories of play and of the good-enough mother.[2]

> Old Mother Hubbard
> Went to the cupboard,
> To fetch her poor dog a bone
> But when she came there
> The cupboard was bare
> And so the poor dog had none.
>
> She went to the baker's
> To buy him some bread;
> But when she came back
> The poor dog was dead.

> She went to the undertaker's
> To buy him a coffin;
> But when she came back
> The poor dog was laughing.

The first six lines are the best known; like many favorite rhymes, it offers a tiny, two-character drama in memorable sounds and thumping rhythms. Apparently this verse and the two succeeding ones were already part of English oral tradition by the time a version of them appeared in print, set to music in 1797 and mentioning "children" rather than "dog" (Opie 377). The rhyme of "coffin" and "laughing" suggests that the verses come from 17th rather than 18th century English. In 1805 these verses and eleven more were published in a little book, *The Comic Adventures of Old Mother Hubbard and Her Dog*, by Sarah Catherine Martin. In these succeeding verses, which became wildly popular as soon as the book appeared, Mother Hubbard attends in various ways to her "child's" needs, while the "child" plays tricks:

> She took a clean dish
> To get him some tripe;
> But when she came back
> He was smoking a pipe.
>
> She went to the alehouse
> To get him some beer;
> But when she came back
> The dog sat in a chair.
>
> She went to the tavern
> For white wine and red;
> But when she came back
> The dog stood on his head.
>
> She went to the fruiterer's
> To buy him some fruit;
> But when she came back
> He was playing the flute.
>
> She went to the tailor's
> To buy him a coat;
> But when she came back
> He was riding a goat.

She went to the hatter's
To buy him a hat,
But when she came back
He was feeding the cat.

She went to the barber's
To buy him a wig;
But when she came back
He was dancing a jig.

She went to the cobbler's
To buy him some shoes;
But when she came back
He was reading the news.

She went to the seamstress
To buy him some linen;
But when she came back
The dog was a-spinning.

She went to the hosier's
To buy him some hose;
But when she came back
He was dressed in his clothes.

The dame made a curtsy,
The dog made a bow;
The dame said, Your servant,
The dog said, Bow-wow.

It is my contention that part of the keen pleasure of these verses for both adult and child is the repeated pattern of a woman going and coming, bringing food and clothing to a creature who remains in one place. They seem to describe one of the earliest human memories in our culture: the infant's locomotor helplessness and the contrasting mobility of the mother, her face appearing, disappearing, reappearing as she cares for its bodily needs—an English folk precursor to the famous *fort/da* game in Freud's *Beyond the Pleasure Principle* (1920).

Freud observed that his grandson never cried when his mother left him alone, but that he especially enjoyed playing at making objects "disappear" and "reappear," repeating an "oh" sound—which his mother interpreted as *fort* ("gone")—when he hid them, and "*Da!*" ("there") joyfully when he found them (14–16). Freud believed the pleasure in the game resulted from the boy's taking a situation in which he was passive—the mother's departure—and repeating it as a game, thereby making himself an active participant, as do children who learn to play "peekaboo."

The popularity of this rhyme, as it was written by Sarah Catherine Martin in 1805, suggests that it taps into a complex set of memories and pleasures for a great many people. It is interesting that a very similar rhyme was published in 1803: "Old Dame Trot and her Comical Cat." In this rhyme, an old woman seeks food for her cat; she finds none, visits the butcher's, and returns to find the cat "dead at her feet." Dame Trot then goes to the undertaker's, returns to find the cat alive after all, and then cares for it through eleven more verses.

According to the Opies, this rhyme was probably well known in some version years before it saw print; certainly Sarah Catherine Martin would have known it. Yet, derivative as it was, and unlike "Old Dame Trot," "Old Mother Hubbard" was a phenomenal success, selling "upwards of ten thousand copies" in a few months, and reprinted, pirated, copied, illustrated, parodied, and expanded by anonymous versifiers many times over right through today. Why did it have greater appeal than "Dame Trot"?

Three seemingly small changes probably account, at least psychoanalytically, for the difference. With the shift from "Dame" to "Mother," the focus of the rhyme moved from wifehood to motherhood, with all the attendant, shared ambivalence and complexities of that state and with greater appropriateness for a child's rhyme. Although "Trot" humorously describes the old woman's running here and yon, the rhyming of "Hubbard" (a name already known in folklore in 1805) with "cupboard" calls up images of kitchens, enclosed spaces, food, and eventually, if unconsciously, the womb and breasts of a mother's body. Further, the shift from a "comical cat" to a dog opens the rhyme to more associations with mothers and children. Cats are known, in English and American pet-keeping, for their independence. They gather their own food, clean themselves, defend themselves from predators, and act as predators themselves even as kittens. Dogs, on the other hand, have for centuries been regarded almost as children in English and American pet-keeping households—petted, scolded, made to obey, fed from the table, generally encouraged to act as dependents. Moreover, the dog traditionally is male, the cat female. "Dame Trot" then centers around two female characters, while "Mother Hubbard" offers a gender balance of male and female. These changes, in my view, gave Sarah Catherine Martin's version greater resonance with unconscious memories and desires.

The first two verses suggest that the dog is merely a dog, and a hungry one, who dies without being fed. He is a "poor" dog, worthy of sympathy. But the third verse, in which the mother arranges for his coffin, takes a surprising turn: the dog is thoroughly alive and laughing—perhaps with pleasure, but also perhaps because he pulled a fast one on his mother. We no longer pity the fellow. Instead we may be a little alarmed, surprised, amused, and vaguely discomfited that he is not so innocent as he appeared. The succeeding verses provide a rollicking description of more tricks, more play. Every time the mother does something for him, his response is indirect at best; he seems mostly to ignore her efforts. The repeated conjunction "But" emphasizes the contrast between the mother's purposeful behavior and the dog's random silliness. In fact, these interior verses, all thirteen of them, can be rearranged in any order, at least from the standpoint of the dog's activities, because what he does is not caused so much by the mother's actual gift to him, but by its *sound*. The rhyme creates the act—tripe/pipe, coat/goat, shoes/news, etc.—in jubilant creative play that delights in itself.

Winnicott believed play was "the universal" in developmental psychology; it "belongs to health," it facilitates health, it is "the natural thing" (*Playing and Reality* 41). Play is the origin of all cultural activity; a child's make-believe becomes a novel, a painting, a symphony. When a child or an adult loses the ability to play, healthy growth stops. Earlier analysts, Melanie Klein and her followers, emphasized play as a treatment tool for psychoanalysis, a window into the child's psyche as dreams are into the adult's. Winnicott made play important for its own sake. Having begun his professional life as a pediatrician, he had observed and played with many babies and children himself. It was the primary way communication began with a child. From his experience he developed his theories of transitional objects and transitional space which first appeared in the 1950s.

In Winnicott's theory, a mother and baby played together in a special psychic space which was neither interior nor exterior, neither real nor symbolic, but a place of transition between them—that is, between mother and baby and between the real world and the imagined one, between interior life and exterior life . He also called it "potential" space—a term which captures its sense of possibility and its power. In this paradoxical place, the child plays while the mother joins in the play, letting the child guide her and giving it a sense of control and omnipotence to balance its otherwise dependent physical life. If the mother is able to do this over time—as Winnicott believed most are—the child will play creatively and eventually be able to say "I AM, I am alive, I am myself" (*Playing and Reality* 56).[3]

In "Old Mother Hubbard," the dog plays in that potential space. Some of the things he does imitate grown-up life: smoking a pipe, reading the news. Some are silly: he stands on his head, rides a goat. He is artistic—plays the flute and dances a jig. He seems masculine, with the pipe and newspaper—and the phallic goat, perhaps. He seems feminine: he feeds the cat and spins. He does these things in no particular order; they are not particularly chaotic, wicked, or destructive activities, at least from the mother's reaction. They seem, if anything, spontaneous, just aimed at keeping Old Mother Hubbard off balance, perhaps a payback for her leaving him (as most mothers have experienced from time to time). But she accepts them and moves on to the next thing.

This is the key element in all the revisions, copies, and new verses, and in most of the illustrations which accompany the rhyme, old and new: the mother's surprise quickly becomes calm acceptance—certainly a perfect image of the good mother, from the child's point of view, and one key element in the mother's role in the potential space she shares with her child.

Winnicott's formulation of the transitional object has become his most famous contribution to psychoanalytic theory. Linus's blanket, in the Charles Schultz comic strip *Peanuts*, is a popular interpretation of it, although Winnicott himself was reluctant to give specific examples because of the wide variety of possibilities. It is an object chosen by the child at about the time the child is beginning to separate from the mother. It represents that "transition." The object, like the mother who is becoming separate from the child, is both loved and hated. It may become dirty and smelly but must never be washed. It may be mistreated—poked, torn, thrown in the dirt, beaten—yet it must be present when the child goes to sleep. A teddy bear, a piece of string, an old blanket may all serve the child in this way, and its ultimate goal is to be discarded when the child has completed the transition from "the state of being merged with the mother to a state of being in relation to the mother as something outside and separate" (*Playing and Reality* 14–15).

Mother Hubbard's dog/child seems to have no single transitional object. He plays randomly with a pipe, flute, goat, cat, spinning wheel. But Winnicott once commented that the object itself is not the issue: "what I am referring to in this part of my work is not the cloth or teddy bear that the baby uses—not so much the object used as the use of the object" (*Playing and Reality* xi–xii). The objects in the rhyme do seem to function as some kind of substitute: "Since you're not here, Mom, since you've gone and left me again, I'll just find something else that pleases me." By the last verse, he is able to discard the objects and get "dressed in his clothes" to address his mother directly, as "something outside and separate," instead of through his use of the objects. They have served their purpose.

For Winnicott, the theory of transitional objects and space was his attempt to focus on the paradox of the child's play: it simultaneously expresses dependence and independence, need and rejection, the real world and the symbolic one. He asked for this paradox to be "accepted and tolerated and respected, and for it not to be resolved" (*Playing and Reality* xii). The closing verse of "Old Mother Hubbard" offers a marvelous image of the paradox: the dog, dressed in human clothes, bows: the mother says to him, with lovely irony, "Your servant," to which his only response is "Bow-wow." Dog/man, child/adult, animal/human, male/female, genteel language/barking—the number of contrasting elements held in equal suspension in the space of four tiny lines of poetry is a triumph of acceptance, tolerance, and respect for paradox.

But is Old Mother Hubbard a good mother? Since the mother of the fifteen-verse poem, the popular one, was invented around 1805, it might be interesting to compare her with another famous mother who was invented in 1801 for a children's story. This was the period when the rational moralists held sway in English-speaking culture. Taking their cue from Locke's theories but still grounded in the moralism of the Puritan attitude toward children, they believed children should be carefully taught that rational behavior *is* moral behavior: if you understood that playing with matches was physically dangerous, then you would obey your mother when she told you not to do it and reap all the rewards of being a good child. If you made a bad choice and did something dangerous or silly, then you would not only be punished by the consequences of it but by your disappointed parents as well.

Maria Edgeworth's famous story "The Purple Jar" tells of Rosamond, a little girl who chooses a purple flower vase, instead of the new shoes she needs, and suffers the irritating and humiliating consequences. It's a pleasant, lively little story, and Rosamond is an unusually believable little girl in comparison with characters in much of the other popular literature of the day. The mother is a perfect representation of the rational moralist notion of the good mother. She responds to Rosamond's questions and desires with carefully calibrated answers and suggestions, attempting to lead her toward the understanding that the jar will not be as useful as the shoes. She does not tell Rosamond that the jar is not really purple; she only asks her to think about its ultimate usefulness. She makes her choose between jar and shoes, saying that she will have to live with her shabby shoes for a month if she chooses the jar. She does not particularly sympathize with Rosamond's tears upon finding the jar is not purple but plain glass: "No, Rosamond, you must abide by your own choice, and now the best thing you can possibly do is to bear your disappointment with good humour" (145).

To today's readers, she seems cold-hearted and manipulative; at one point, she plants the idea of the jar in Rosamond's head after the child has forgotten about her desire for it, almost as if she wants to get her daughter into hot water. And she does not relent, even after Rosamond's shoes are sole-less. But to readers of 1805, she used a situation of the child's choosing to teach her an important lesson. She was a good rational moralist mother—but probably more an ideal than a reality.

Old Mother Hubbard seems a rather gentler version of a good rational moralist mother. Most of her actions involve providing for her child's physical needs—food and clothing. In contrast to the dog's activities, hers seem less random. The early half of the poem concerns food and drink, and the second half concerns clothing. From what we can see, she keeps at her activities steadily, despite the dog's silliness, caring for him and at the same time encouraging him to progress. The food choices seem to grow more sophisticated: bread, tripe, beer, wine, fruit. And the clothing choices pile up: coat, hat, wig, shoes, linen (underclothes), and hose.

Winnicott's good-enough mother at first mirrors her child's desires as closely as possible and satisfies them, then gradually begins to help the child realize that it cannot always have its desires satisfied completely, immediately. She begins to disillusion the child; it is not omnipotent after all, not in complete control of reality. She has a life too, apart from the child. She leaves, but always returns. In this way, she gradually builds up the child's ability to tolerate frustration and to deal with it in imagination. She constantly nudges the child toward greater responsibility and maturity, while at the same time providing security.

That Mother Hubbard has been successful at this process is suggested by the last two verses: when she returns with the hose, she finds him "dressed in his clothes"—finally a direct response to her actions, not random play. Her constant care, her constant returning, has made him able to achieve some maturity. Her response is then to treat him even more like a grown-up: she curtsies to him and says, "Your servant"—a polite greeting of the day (which of course has interesting ironies since she has been acting as a servant to her "baby"). His response is also direct: he bows, and acknowledges her greeting. But of course the joke is that he is still a dog—or child, depending on where we are in this metaphor—and can't talk. She may not be omnipotent, but she still has language on her side.

These mothers—Rosamond's and Mother Hubbard herself—represent an ideal of motherhood that seems to tally with the rational moralist attitude of the early 1800s, minus some of the overtly manipulative tactics that the attitude admits at times. They demonstrate that motherhood is, as one analyst put it, "a thoughtful skill—a nurturant letting-be—based on judgment and requiring confidence in the child's potential" (First 151). This is Winnicott's good-enough mother.

However, Winnicott was not writing in the early 1800s but in the late 1940s and 1950s, post–Freud and post–World War II, when acknowledgments of human ambivalence and potential for cruelty were becoming more open and child-care manuals were adopting a sensible tone.[4] So Winnicott's good-enough mother has another side: she hates her baby at the same time that she loves it. The word hate may seem overly strong, but it is necessary to establish that this feeling on the mother's part is a genuine ambivalence; only hate can balance the love she feels simultaneously. And she must bear the hate especially "without doing anything about it…. The most remarkable thing about a mother is her ability to be hurt by her baby and to hate it so much without paying the child out, and her ability to wait for rewards that may or may not come at a later date" ("Hate in the Countertransference" 202).

Winnicott created a remarkable list of the reasons why a mother "hates her baby from the word go." I reproduce part of it here:

> The baby is a danger to her body in pregnancy and at birth.
> The baby is an interference to her private life, a challenge to preoccupation.
> The baby hurts her nipples by suckling, which is at first a chewing activity.
> He is ruthless, treats her as scum, an unpaid servant, a slave.
> She has to love him, excretions and all, at any rate at the beginning, till he has doubts about himself.
> He tries to hurt her, periodically bites her, all in love.
> He shows disillusionment about her.
> His excited love is cupboard love, so that having got what he wants he throws her away like orange peel.
> He is suspicious, refuses her good food, and makes her doubt herself, but eats well with his aunt.
> After an awful morning with him she goes out, and he smiles at a stranger, who says, "Isn't he sweet?"
> If she fails him at the start she knows he will pay her out for ever ["Hate in the Countertransference" 201].

Winnicott's experience as a pediatrician is seldom more obvious than in this list; he has seen many mothers in their best and worst moments, and knows that the kind of hate they feel is not evil nor destructive, but a compound of exasperation, responsibility, and fatigue.

Rozsika Parker's wonderfully readable book on maternal ambivalence, *Mother Love/Mother Hate* makes a strong case for the creative outcome of such paradoxical feelings. It is at moments such as the ones Winnicott describes that good-enough mothers turn to singing rhymes such as "Rockabye baby" or "Baa baa black sheep," or "Old Mother Hubbard," or to humming or knee bouncing or soothing with bottle, breast, holding, stroking, or pacifier—all these creative acts to contain the momentary surge of hatred. Even the most fleeting acknowledgment to herself of the hate she feels can help her to control it.

Parker, writing in 1995, also points out that a mother's ambivalence does not arise solely through her own physical or psychic response to her baby. It is encouraged in textbooks on mothering, advertisements for cereals, radio and television programs, bumper stickers—the whole panoply of popular culture which offers impossible ideals of Good Mothers, not just Winnicott's good-enough mothers. In fact, Parker believes that as increasing numbers of mothers work outside the home and lead more complex and mobile lives, the public representations of the Good Mother have become more dogmatic rather than less so (2).

On television, beautiful women in white negligees cuddle beautiful healthy babies in spotlessly clean, soft-focus rooms. The mothers we see in magazine and television ads smile wryly when a toddler spills chocolate milk on the white carpet, then clean it up with the greatest efficiency and good humor. TV parents play with their children like children themselves, then dispense sage advice or loving maternal care like intelligent adults. They seem always to know when to hold on, and when to let go. The deep ambivalence that troubles most real-life mothers seems never to have touched them. And real-life mothers constantly absorb the image, test themselves against it, and find themselves wanting, even while they participate in re-creating it by buying the products and adopting a public behavior that imitates it.

In my view, this situation accounts for the popularity of *Love You Forever*, written in 1986 by Robert Munsch and illustrated by Sheila McGraw. This popular little book resembles "Old Mother Hubbard" in a general way. Both trace out a two-person drama of mothering and maturation, and both rely on repetitive language patterns for their chief effects. In fact, the text of *Love You Forever* works much better on its own, without the illustrations, because of its resemblance to an orally-transmitted folktale.[5] But though it was published as a children's book, I think it is bought and enjoyed mostly by mothers, because it adopts the same tone as all those television commercials and sitcoms.

Mothers can appreciate its momentary comic exasperation at her child's misbehavior—"Sometimes his mother wanted to sell him to the zoo!"—and immediately suppresses this little slip by embracing the book's completely unambivalent refrain: "I'll love you forever, I'll like you for always, As long as I'm living my baby you'll be." This is accompanied by images, in the words and pictures, of a grown woman crawling across the floor while her child sleeps, to hold and rock him even when he is a "great big man," and sing her unambivalent lullaby.

While this image certainly arouses comforting fantasies of mother love continuing as we sleep, I wonder whether children might find the image of a grown woman sneaking up on them in the middle of the night—and pursuing them this way even into adulthood—puzzling or disturbing, even on a symbolic level. It suggests that we can never escape the omnipotent mother—a fantasy more appealing to adults than to children.

Toward the end of the book, the son comforts the aging mother, holding her on his lap and singing the same refrain—another image that might make children uncomfortable. It might be seen as a hint that the mother who shares this book with her child expects the same treatment—rather a large burden to place on a child who has trouble foreseeing his own growth much less his parents' aging. The closing moment shows the father singing the lullaby to his own baby, a suggestion that unambivalent love engenders more unambivalent love.

The book reflects the pressures put on good-enough mothers—by themselves and by the culture—to be not just better mothers but to be the Good Mother of the archetypal ideal. But every archetype stands directly beside its opposite: the notion of the Good Mother implies that there is also a Bad Mother with equal and opposite characteristics. The intensity of the love in *Love You Forever* makes me wonder about the repressed ambivalence of the mothers who enjoy it. What notion of a bad mother is implied by such a good mother? Our culture has plenty of input here. "At risk" children have become an entire industry, and mothers are usually to blame. Stephanie Coontz puts it best:

> If you stayed too long in the Jacuzzi or took a couple of drinks during pregnancy, your baby is "at risk" for learning disabilities. It you failed to bond with your infant in the critical early months or even minutes, your child is "at risk" for insecure attachment. If you put your boy in a certain kind of day care at a particular age, he is "at risk"; if you don't put your girl in the same kind of day care at the same age, she is "at risk." If you are divorced, your kids are "at risk."

If you and your spouse stayed together for the sake of the kids and couldn't hide the tension, then they are still "at risk." And if your own behavior hasn't put your kids at risk, their future is threatened by the parents who *have* ruined their kids, causing the rise in crime and the disintegration of our schools [209].

The guilt heaped upon mothers, and the guilt mothers heap upon themselves, today is enormous.

In 1957, Winnicott spoke about society's debt to mothers. Emphasizing that he did not mean gratitude for being born or for supplying a home or for helping children become home-builders, he said that "every man or woman who is sane, every man or woman who has the feeling of being a person in the world, and for whom the world means something, every happy person, is in infinite debt to a woman" ("Mother's Contribution" 125). On the face of it this sounds like the kind of "Good Mother" talk we hear around Mother's Day. But Winnicott was a psychoanalyst and his perspective more complex than that. He went on to say that the result of such recognition "will be a lessening in ourselves of a fear ... a vague fear of dependence." From the beginning of life, when we literally owe our survival to a woman, we fear a return to such absolute dependence—not a return to Woman, as some have thought, but the fear of dependence, which may wear a woman's face but which is our own fear, male or female.

Perhaps the image of the old woman in her son's arms assuages the fear of dependence in mothers who enjoy *Love You Forever*, but it may exacerbate such fears in a child reader. I think the reason I am disturbed by the book is that, to me, it trades on our fear of dependence. In my view, a healthier image, and a more satisfying one for children, is the closing image of "Old Mother Hubbard," in which the mother and child meet standing politely on almost equal ground, respecting each other as individuals but acknowledging their differences. The mother has allowed dependence, while nudging her child toward independence.

In Rozsika Parker's many interviews with ordinary good-enough mothers, what emerged was not a desire for oneness with their babies but for "loving moments of at oneness"—mutuality rather than unity (23–48). In *Love You Forever*, the refrain is sung when the child is sleeping—not enjoying a mutual experience. Their mutual experience comes only later when the mother is dying. Old Mother Hubbard and her dog/child look each other in the eye and acknowledge their moment of mutuality. This, I believe, is the ultimate triumph of the ordinary good-enough mother.

Notes

1. Some feminist thinkers have taken Winnicott to task for his "good-enough mother" concept for several reasons. It seems to assume that the mothering is always done by a female and that the mother is always mothering full-time while the child is an infant. It seems to ignore environmental differences and cultural differences, and apparently pays no attention to the difference between a mother's response to a boy child and a girl child. Winnicott did address these issues in a transient way throughout his work, but Claire Kahane, for example, in "Gender and Voice in Transitional Phenomena" (1993), notes that although Winnicott was trying to avoid setting up an impossible ideal, this is what he, in fact, did.

2. Part of this essay was published in Lucy Rollin, *Cradle and All* (1992).

3. This is the signal achievement in human psychological life—the knowledge of who we are in relation to others, but it is a knowledge that is always a little shaky, always being tested on the line between interior and exterior reality. That is why adults still need creative play.

4. In the United States, Dr. Benjamin Spock, influenced by Winnicott, was writing his famous *Baby and Child Care*.

5. I am indebted to Tony Tallent, graduate student at the University of North Carolina at Charlotte in 1998, for this insight.

Works Cited

Coontz, Stephanie. *The Way We Never Were.* New York: Basic Books, 1992.

Edgeworth, Maria. "The Purple Jar." In *From Instruction to Delight*, Ed. Patricia Demers and Gordon Moyles. Toronto: Oxford University Press, 1982.

First, Elsa. "Mothering, Hate, and Winnicott." In *Representations of Motherhood.* Ed. Bassin, Honey, and Kaplan. New Haven: Yale University Press, 1994.

Freud, Sigmund. *Beyond the Pleasure Principle* (1920). In vol. 18 of *The Standard Edition of the Complete Psycological Works of Sigmund Freud*. Trans. James Strachey. 24 vols. London: Hogarth, 1955.

Kahane, Claire. "Gender and Voice in Transitional Phenomena." In *Transitional Objects and Potential Spaces: Literary Uses of D. W. Winnicott.* Ed. Peter Rudnytsky. New York: Columbia University Press, 1993.

Munsch, Robert. *Love You Forever.* Illus. Sheila McGraw. Willowdale, Ontario: Firefly Books, 1986.

Opie, Iona and Peter. *The Oxford Dictionary of Nursery Rhymes*, 2nd edition. Oxford: Oxford University Press, 1997.

Parker, Rozsika. *Mother Love/Mother Hate.* New York: Basic Books, 1995.

Rollin, Lucy. *Cradle and All.* Jackson: University Press of Mississippi, 1992.

Winnicott, D. W. "Hate in the Countertransference." In *Through Pediatrics to Psychoanalysis.* New York: Basic Books, 1958.

Winnicott, D. W. "The Mother's Contribution to Society." In *Home Is Where We Start From.* New York: W. W. Norton, 1986.

Winnicott, D. W. *Playing and Reality* (1971). New York: Routledge, 1989.

CHAPTER 11

Humpty Dumpty and the Anxieties of the Vulnerable Child

Lucy Rollin

> Humpty Dumpty sat on a wall;
> Humpty Dumpty had a great fall;
> All the king's horses
> And all the king's men
> Couldn't put Humpty together again.

This little rhyme, one of the most popular and familiar in the entire canon of nursery rhymes, is so old that scholars have speculated that its age could be measured in thousands of years. English-speaking children and adults share it with a number of other languages as well: Humpty is Boule-Boule in France, Lille-Trille in Denmark, Gigele-Gagele or Runtzelkin-Puntselkin in different parts of Germany, to cite only a few of his other names. What all of these share is the riddling nature of the rhyme, and the answer to the riddle is always the same: an egg.

But most of us know that isn't the whole answer. Eggs don't sit on walls; people sit on walls. Illustrators who have addressed the rhyme have invariably created a humanized egg (Maxfield Parrish evidently enjoyed the subject), or, as in the case of Kate Greenaway, simply drawn a child on a wall. The term Humpty Dumpty was used in 1785 to describe a "short clumsy person of either sex"—a phrase that could certainly describe the way most children see themselves and the way adults remember themselves as children. In fact, though Lewis Carroll's Humpty says to Alice, "It's very provoking to be called an egg—very," the popularity and wide acceptance of the metaphor imbedded in this rhyme suggests that most of us are quite willing to think of ourselves as egg-like.

The question is, why should this rhyme, which not only encourages us to think of ourselves as eggs, first in a very precarious position but then as irretrievably destroyed eggs, be enjoyable? In this paper I offer a psycho-analytic explanation: because the rhyme allows us to express and contain the most basic human anxieties in a single highly compressed metaphor: a falling egg. And in so doing it allows us to contemplate and even, at some level, to remember that anxiety while acknowledging our mastery of it.

Several analysts have used the rhyme specifically to describe anxiety in their patients. Thomas A. Petty in 1953 noted that the rhyme drama-tizes the "second catastrophic trauma a child experiences: viz., the arrival of a sibling" (412), and presented clinical evidence from three cases. In the first, a four-year-old boy, after his younger brother had almost fallen into the fireplace, batted a Humpty Dumpty balloon with a broom, balancing it on the fire screen and catching it when it nearly fell in; later, while vying with his brother for his mother' attention, he bit into the balloon, punc-turing it and destroying it.

In the second case, a two-year-old boy had a Humpty Dumpty doll, definitely identified with his younger brother, which he handled roughly and eventually stuffed into a mailbox, evidently trying to undo the sibling's birth. Petty's third analysand, an adult, also had a younger brother; he dreamed of sitting on a wall and triumphantly throwing down an egg-shaped object with great force. This patient mentioned that the rhyme had recurred to him many times over the years without apparent reason; in analysis he came to feel it definitely represented to him the anger he felt toward his brother.

Petty felt that for each of these patients, the egg and the fall repre-sented both the first-born child and the second: for the first, the analysand, the falling egg represented the irreparable damage done to his relationship with his parents by the sibling's birth; the broken egg represented the new child destroyed in fantasy. To Petty, the rhyme was a valuable therapeutic tool for these patients; its form allowed the "attenuated repetition of severe psychic trauma" and then its mastery. As with many other rhymes, its very simplicity lends itself to the symbolic expression of infantile conflict (405).

Renato J. Almansi, a practicing analyst and editor of *American Imago*, found in his early practice a similar use of the metaphor of the falling egg.

His patient, aged 26, also had a younger brother. In the course of deciphering a screen memory associated with the day of his brother's birth, the patient suddenly remembered an incident which had taken place a few months before his brother's birth, when the patient was four and a half. Always a good boy, he had nevertheless, that day, found a basket of eggs in the kitchen, dragged the basket to a chair, climbed onto the table with the basket, and one by one, watching intently, dropped the eggs onto the floor.

This story was told many times in his family since it was so out of character for him. In analysis, Almansi asked him whether he remembered at the time what he knew about eggs; he promptly replied that he knew very well that chicks came from eggs. Almansi speculates that the egg-breaking spree represented an investigative attitude—a "ferment of mental questioning, debating and hypothesizing" as the child attempted to imagine the "exact mechanisms of the birth process" (39). Like Petty, Almansi finds the rhyme a "ready-made metaphor for the feelings of an older child who feels displaced by a newcomer and may, therefore, very easily work itself into the production of certain patients who are having trouble along such lines" (42). This particular child had been told that babies come in packages, but he evidently figured out for himself, to a considerable degree, the truth.

Whether or not the birth of a sibling triggers it, children are intensely curious about the birth process. It seems to them to be the riddle that never gets answered, and probably, in fact, remains one of the most mysterious elements of life for all of us—a common physiological event of the most transcendent significance for which the mystery of the egg is a perfect symbol. The Humpty Dumpty rhyme is a riddle similar to others among the rhymes:

> As I was walking in a field of wheat:,
> I picked up something good to eat;
> Neither fish, flesh, fowl, nor bone,
> I kept it till it ran alone.
>
> In marble halls as white as milk,
> Lined with a skin as soft as silk,
> Within a fountain crystal clear,
> A golden apple doth appear.
> No doors are there to this stronghold,
> Yet thieves break in and steal the gold.

These riddles share with Humpty Dumpty the notion of something valuable that irretrievably changes. What it does not share with them is the notion of falling; this element seems crucial to the rhyme's popularity and I will return to it. What I wish to stress here is that, just as parents are reluctant to talk to children about birth—probably because its mystery finally baffles us—scientists and analysts have seemed to ignore it as well, leaving it the riddle that never gets answered.

The most notable exception was Otto Rank. In his now-infamous book *The Trauma of Birth*, he advanced the theory that the biological separation of the infant from the mother at birth was the root of all later anxiety, a kind of Ur-trauma, as Peter Gay puts it, that could provide analysts with a therapeutic key. But analysts then and now are uncomfortable with his emphasis on the physiological aspects of birth over the metaphoric ones. In his response to Rank—*Inhibitions, Symptoms, and Anxiety* (1926)—Freud speculated that birth was the prototype of the anxiety reaction, but at the same time tended to discard the importance of the individual birth in favor of a more phylogenetic approach.

In the mid 1940s, as she began her work in this area, Phyllis Greenacre in *Trauma, Growth, and Personality* noted that serious scientific material seemed to focus on the fetus "right up to the time of birth," and then focus on the problems of the neonate, without "daring to look at" the effect of birth itself. She commented, "Perhaps birth is inevitably too close to death in our feelings; perhaps the struggle of birth is at once too terrifying and too inspiring for us to regard it readily with scientific dispassion. Perhaps men have too much exclusion anxiety and women too much direct anxiety" (14–15). I personally think it is no accident that a female analyst—Greenacre—and an unusual pediatrician—D. W. Winnicott—have been the two analysts to face these ideas most directly, without minimizing their riddling mysteries.

Greenacre and Winnicott both speak of the birth *experience*, as opposed to the birth trauma. Both analysts found, in the course of their work, considerable evidence that birth experiences are held as memory material. Greenacre was able, at times, to gain from adult dreams and symptoms an idea of the special birth experience of the individual and her reconstruction "sometimes proved rather surprisingly correct" (Almansi 47). She found that certain head sensations and headaches reactivated in periods of stress could be correlated with the form of birth experience of the individual. She also found in her research that "cerebral injury resulting from birth is very much more common than one might suppose" (41). She commented, "It does seem strange … that the head, containing the most precious heritage, the well-developed cerebrum, should not only be the cause of much of the stress of birth but that it is, at the same time, the very part of the infant most endangered during birth" (56). Such findings bear out the rhyme's emphasis on fragility and suggest that the many illustrations which make Humpty's egg-shaped head one with his whole body may be responding metaphorically to the genuine risk to the head in birth, and to the anxiety that accompanies this memory trace.

In his work, Winnicott found that constrictions of the head and chest and the experience of being unable to breathe were psychosomatic sensations related to the birth experience, as was the less traumatic sensation of the whole body as propulsive object. And like Greenacre, he found that certain analysands were able to bring memory traces of their births into the analysis (*Through Pediatrics* 180).

In his paper on birth experience, Winnicott defines anxiety as the feeling of being in the "grips of a physical experience ... [which one] can neither avoid nor understand" (*Through Pediatrics* 181). In a later paper, he commented that it is helpful to think of the normal infant as an "immature being always on the brink of unthinkable anxiety," and outlined the four varieties of "unthinkable anxiety": going to pieces and falling forever are the first two (*Maturational* 58). The symbolism of falling is of course highly complex, as popular metaphors indicate: we fall in love, fall asleep, fall from grace, and fall out with an acquaintance. Margaret Mahler speculates that its importance arises from that crucial period in a child's life when it begins to walk (222). But poet Samuel Coleridge—and the most popular lullaby in English—associate falling with something much earlier: the loss of the maternal touch. In Coleridge's notebooks, he comments, "Sense of diminished contact explains falling asleep—this is fear" (Durham 177).

The Humpty Dumpty metaphor offers an image not only of falling but falling to certain disaster—of going to pieces, one of the deepest anxieties of the immature being. Winnicott's other "unthinkable anxieties" are having no relationship to the body and having no orientation (*Maturational* 58), which also suggest the neonate's condition. This Gordian knot of images, so difficult to describe separately, fuse in the image of the falling egg to depict the physiological and metaphoric moment of birth: a moment of complete exposure, fragility, hope, and despair.

Australian analyst Isla Lonie has cited material—from one of his most painful cases—which illustrates how such unthinkable anxiety can persist negatively into adult life. His 29-year-old patient, who had never experienced loving human relationships and had spent most of her life in hospitals, constantly cut and injured herself, saying to him, "There is nothing you can do to mend this broken egg-shell," and crying out, "I am Humpty Dumpty!" As a child, she remembered, she was always "on the brink of terror." Her ego, says Lonie, had an "egg-shell quality"; all her potential was "still at the level of yolk and albumen" (378). For such a patient, Lonie believes the theories of Winnicott, which reach back toward earliest childhood and analyze preverbal material while providing a holding environment, were the only useful therapeutic possibilities.

For most of us, though, as the popularity of this rhyme indicates, calling ourselves Humpty Dumpty gives pleasure, even while it calls up what may be somatic memory traces of unthinkable anxiety. For the metaphor works not only for the physical event of birth but the psychic one as well. Winnicott uses the term "Humpty Dumpty stage" to describe the moment in infantile life when the baby recognizes the mother as separate—a precarious moment. "No longer devotedly held," the child must now balance an inner and an outer life; otherwise it is "liable to irreversible disintegration" (*Through Pediatrics* 226; *Maturational* 75). Since most of us survived that precarious perch and went on to become integrated human beings, saying this rhyme becomes an affirmation of our success at the same time that it lets us remember what might have happened.

But popular culture has never needed an analyst to tell us that reliving such an event metaphorically is life-affirming. Iona and Peter Opie describe a girls' parlor game called "Humpty Dumpty" which was played in 1883: girls sit down holding their skirts tightly about their feet; at and an agreed signal, they all fall backwards and then must recover their balance without letting go of their skirts (215). They comment that this game might be older than the rhyme: No doubt. If any further proof were needed of the sophisticated bricolage that characterizes folk rhymes and game, this game, with its associations of falling, sexual activity, females, eggs, and perhaps even the prevention of pregnancy, should provide it.

Freud once commented that there was a point in every dream where the images become too enmeshed to analyze; he called this the "navel" of the dream. In this sense, Humpty Dumpty is the "navel" of the nursery rhymes, compressing all our memories and fantasies about isolation, value, birth, falling, destruction, hope, infancy, and survival into its single metaphor of the falling egg, where they become too intertwined to tease apart, and where we can experience them without analyzing away their wonder and mystery.

Works Cited

Almansi, Renato J. "Humpty Dumpty: Some Speculations on the Nursery Rhyme."
    American Imago 43 (1986): 35–49.

Carroll, Lewis. *Through the Looking Glass*. In *The Annotated Alice*. Ed. Martin Gardner. New York: Bramhall House, 1960.

Durham, Margery. "The Mother Tongue: *Christabel* and the Language of Love." In *The (M)other Tongue*. Eds. Garner, Kahane, Sprengnether. 169–193. Ithaca, NY: Cornell University Press, 1985.

Freud, Sigmund. *Inhibitions, Symptoms, and Anxiety*. (1926). In vol. 20 of *The Standard Edition of the Complete Psychological Works of Sigmund Freud*. Trans. James Strachey. 24 vols. London: Hogarth, 1959.

Greenacre, Phyllis. "The Biological Economy of Birth" and "The Predisposition to Anxiety." In *Trauma, Growth and Personality*. New York: International Universities Press, 1952.

Lonie, Isla. "From Humpty Dumpty to Rapunzel." *Australian and New Zealand Journal of Psychiatry* 19 (1985): 372–31.

Mahler, Margaret, Fred Pine, and Anni Bergman. *The Psychological Birth of the Human Infant: Symbiosis and Individuation*. New York: Basic Books, 1975.

Opie, Iona and Peter. *The Oxford Dictionary of Nursery Rhymes*. Oxford: Oxford University Press, 1984.

Petty, Thomas A. "The Tragedy of Humpty Dumpty." *Psychoanalytic Study of the Child* 9 (1953): 404–412.

Rank, Otto. *The Trauma of Birth*. New York: Robert Brunner, 1952.

Winnicott, D. W. *The Maturational Processes and the Facilitating Environment*. Madison, CT.: International Universities Press, 1965.

_____. *Through Pediatrics to Psycho-analysis* (1958). New York: Basic Books, 1975.

CHAPTER 12

Dream Imagery and the Portrayal of Childhood Anxieties in Nursery Rhyme Illustrations

Lucy Rollin

The infantile elements in nursery rhymes are often disturbing to adults. Devouring, violent death, mutilation, the torture of animals, insults, crude jests, omnipotent and threatening mother figures, all remind us, consciously or unconsciously, of early anxieties. Yet artists and book-buyers alike are drawn to this material and take great pleasure in interpretive illustrations of the rhymes. Dreams, too, translate words into pictures, offering the dreamer pleasurable or frightening images that partly reveal, partly conceal dream thoughts.

In this sense, there exists an analogy between dreaming and illustration, since both translate words and ideas into pictures, and both allow the contemplation of forbidden notions through the operation of censoring devices. Of course, there are important differences between dreams and illustrations. Dreams move; illustrations do not. Dreams are private; illustrations are public, especially where nursery rhymes are concerned since they constitute a text that belongs to oral as well as written culture.

Artists make conscious selections based on their particular talents, on previous artists' work, and on the desires of editors. Artists also respond in one degree or another to what the culture feels is appropriate for children. In this respect, illustrations resemble other cultural artifacts which reflect society's image of itself. Nevertheless, the analogy offers a way to analyze a given illustration by exploring how the artist's selection of details creates a pleasurable experience for the viewer.

In his attempt to understand why dreams with otherwise frightening material in them might still be pleasurable, Freud posited a kind of "censor" in our dreaming life. Its duty is to protect the dreamer from too vivid an experience of the disturbing infantile material that gives rise to the dream—that is, to its latent content. The dreamwork, as Freud called it, of this "censor" consists of two tasks in particular: condensation and displacement. In condensation, the dreamer pictures only one or two elements of the dream thoughts instead of the whole complex of fears, wishes, and experiences which gave rise to the dream. The dreamer also fuses several elements into one, as, for example, when we "see" one person in a dream but know it is a combination of several people. In this sense the process is similar to metaphor. Displacement, like metonymy, refers to the replacement of one element with another, shifting what Freud called the "psychical accent" from something important to something unimportant (174). Thus the censor camouflages the latent dream and creates the manifest dream— that which we experience or "see."

Many nursery rhymes may also be said to resemble dreams in that they have both latent and manifest content, their surface nonsense or simple narratives more or less concealing disturbing themes. Humpty Dumpty, for example, tells a brief tale of someone or something falling to complete destruction. The rhythm and rhyme make this story enjoyable to recite, and children in many cultures have recited some form of it for centuries (Opie 215–16). Yet such a recitation implies the contemplation of violent death, perhaps even one's own if one identifies consciously or unconsciously with Humpty Dumpty.

Why the rhyme remains pleasurable, especially to small children, is a question which addresses one of the most puzzling aspects of human nature. Perhaps even more disturbing is a rhyme which is recited (or sung) by mothers to children: "Hushabye Baby." This rhyme, with its soothing sounds and rhythms, rocks a baby and then plunges it to the ground, to injury or death. Yet it may be the single most transmitted rhyme in the canon, offered by mother to infant, generation after generation, for centuries. Why should this rhyme be pleasurable to mothers? Like "Humpty Dumpty," its manifest content might be seen as innocent, perhaps a quaint depiction of early wind-rocked cradles (Opie 61–62), but like "Humpty," its latent content recalls Winnicott's catalogue of the few unthinkable anxieties of infancy: going to pieces, falling forever, having no relation to the body, and having no orientation (*Maturational* 58).

Both of these rhymes require the artist to think about such subliminal anxieties and to reproduce them in some visual form. This dual necessity presents a difficult task for the serious illustrator, who will want to offer an image that is pleasurable and presumably suitable, for children's eyes, while at the same time recording a recognizable personal interpretation of the rhyme. Maurice Sendak finds the rhymes a particular challenge: "No other writing so ruthlessly exposes the illustrator's strengths and inadequacies" (190). Yet many artists have risen to the task.

A sampling of illustrators whose collections have been regularly stocked by bookstores for years (Blanche Fisher Wright and Kate Greenaway, for example), leavened with more recent artists (such as Arnold Lobel and Alan Marks), offers an opportunity to explore the various solutions artists have found. The illustrators treated here represent both British and American, nineteenth and twentieth-century collections, and are balanced between male and female artists who work in a wide variety of styles. The selection is meant to be representative only in the broadest sense, but it does reveal some significant patterns of condensation, in contrast to more idiosyncratic displacement in the details of the images.

Humpty Dumpty is a riddle, the answer to which is an egg. The rhyme makes sense in that a broken egg can never be whole again. Yet there is ample evidence that for several centuries Humpty Dumpty has also referred to a human. The *OED* cites a definition of the term from 1785 — "a short clumsy person of either sex" — as well as a nineteenth-century girls' game called Humpty Dumpty. Iona and Peter Opie also comment that since eggs do not sit on walls, the verse is understandable "if it describes human beings who are personating eggs" (215).

Illustrators of this rhyme generally condense it into a single image: an egg with a few human characteristics sitting, usually in relative security, on a wall. Raymond Briggs' Humpty, in his tiny top hat and large red bow tie, typifies many illustrators' interpretations: he smiles innocuously, the only hint of his impending fall being the slight tilt of his body. Some illustrators focus on Humpty's fall but find ways to disguise the humanity of the egg. Arnold Lobel's Humpty, falling in a series of images superimposed on each other over a double-page spread, has quite a human face that grows more terrified as he falls; upon landing he becomes a completely inhuman heap of eggshell — an ambivalent image. Similarly, Feodor Rojankovsky's Hitler-esque Humpty slips, in three stages, from his wall to become a puddle of yolk and white. While Lobel's "great fall" seems to mean from a great height," Rojankovsky suggests a political and more ironic meaning.

Marguerite de Angeli has made the egg more human. She sketches a lanky child with a large head; he is lying on the grass, a surprised look on his delicate face, the top of his head broken open and its liquid contents spilling out. This small drawing looks almost spontaneous and unfinished, compared to most others in the book, and it is placed off to the side and top of the page, away from the rhyme itself, as if de Angeli (or her editor) were uncertain about it. Sendak described de Angeli's nursery rhyme illustrations as "sweet" and "baby-cute" (193), but this image combines that quality with a depiction of a shattered brain and suggests the fragility of a child's head quite directly. The illustration is a particularly dramatic example of an artist revealing latent content.

Relatively few of the artists I have chosen accent the rhyme's military elements. Indeed, in this rhyme the king's horses and king's men, those symbols of patriarchal or parental power, are impotent. For example, Alan Marks' full-page water color shows a brick wall stretching up off the top of the page. At the very bottom of the page, we see the upper bodies of three soldiers, two looking down in dismay, the third looking up. We do not see what they see, only their bewilderment and their slight foolishness in their powdered wigs and fancy uniforms. Marks' condensed image completely displaces the focus of the rhyme: the broken egg. He does draw, on the next page, a small silhouette of an upside-down falling egg/person, facing away from us. Taken together, these pictures are an excellent example of the artist shifting the "psychical accent" of the rhyme from the falling egg to the bewildered soldiers.

Wallace Tripp also focuses on the king's men and moves away from the egg/human identification. His three-part illustration shows a hand reaching up to place an egg on the battlement of a castle, the egg falling, and in the largest picture, a king with egg yolk on his head glaring at some surprised soldiers. He grumbles, in a speech balloon, "Is this someone's idea of a yolk?" Tripp has made the impotence of the king's horses and men even more ludicrous than Marks has, illustrating Freud's contention that condensation and displacement are as much the province of jokes as of dreams, since both jokes and dreams allow us to express and contemplate in disguise things we ordinarily avoid thinking or talking about. Here, Tripp has completely displaced the elements of human frailty and fear of falling; the king and soldiers are all portrayed as solid-looking animals. What fell was only a literal egg, and the "psychical accent" is on a relatively harmless prank. This illustration thoroughly conceals the anxiety-producing elements latent in this rhyme.

If the rhyme "Humpty Dumpty" implicitly identifies human beings with eggs, then those human beings would most likely be children or infants, since their unformed bodies and large fragile heads are similar to the shape, potentiality, and fragility of an egg.[1] Humpty can represent adults as well; adults may often feel as physically fragile as children, even though they may not be visibly at risk as often as children are. But the notion of a child falling to its destruction is repressed in illustrations depicting Humpty as an adult egg/person, and most illustrations that I examined for this study do so. De Angeli is a notable exception here, as is Kate Greenaway, whose approach to the rhyme is a fascinating blend of condensation and displacement. No doubt Greenaway's choice was governed by her gift for drawing beautiful, quiet children rather than falling eggs, but her depiction is nonetheless dramatic. A small child is sitting on a high wall, legs dangling, leaning slightly forward and gazing pensively into the distance. Aside from a tree in the background, nothing else appears in the picture. Underneath, Greenaway has printed only the first two lines of the rhyme, ending with "had a great fall."

While other artists tend to displace the humanity implied in the rhyme onto an egg, Greenaway's drawing, like de Angeli's, more directly addresses the similarity between a young child and an egg; the rhyme has become more clearly metaphorical and, to my mind, has left the "psychical accent" on the most important latent element—and on the element which I believe accounts for the rhyme's persistence in our culture: a child's fragility.

Like so many other illustrators for children, and in particular illustrators of nursery rhymes including almost all those I examined for this essay, Greenaway creates quaint, old fashioned settings and costumes for her interpretations. Such nostalgia is not only appropriate for the often archaic language of the rhymes, but safely distances artist and viewer alike from their overt or implied violence and physicality. In the case of "Hushabye Baby" (or "Rockabye baby" in some American editions) the cradle itself, much more than Humpty Dumpty's wall, suggests a reference to the past.

Despite this built-in defense, illustrating "Hushabye Baby" may be more challenging to artists than illustrating Humpty Dumpty, psychologically speaking, since the rhyme is manifestly about a falling infant, without the egg disguise. Most of the artists whose pictures I examined avoid showing the fall, and the considerable suggestion of movement in the rhyme—rocking, blowing, breaking, falling—is usually absent, the entire rhyme condensed into a single image of stillness: a baby sleeping securely in a cradle.

Some illustrators displace the baby's insecurity in the rhyme to details of the cradle and the tree. Feodor Rojankovsky's baby smiles out from the hood of a heavy, carved, brightly-painted Bavarian cradle, wedged among the branches of a small, gnarled tree. The cradle looks far too heavy for the tree, and a cat is crouched on the hood. But the heft and solidity of the overall image, and the other friendly animals nearby, balance the rhyme's latent threat. Blanche Fisher Wright's infant also sleeps in a very solid cradle, suspended from the branches of an equally solid tree with sturdy ropes. The threat here is displaced onto the white space under the cradle, space which spills into the margins of the picture when the outline containing the picture abruptly ends (a technique she uses frequently but seldom to such effect). Tasha Tudor's baby lies peacefully in a heavy wooden cradle, but among the thinnest branches and most delicate leaves, stretched out into pale blue space under a crescent moon.

Some artists convey the baby's precarious situation by using baskets rather than cradles. De Angeli again contributes an unusual image. Her baby is awake and playing in a laundry basket suspended from a solid limb; unlike most other babies nestled deep in their cradles, this one lies atop her blankets, arms and legs waving free. The sweetness of the baby's face and body soften the implied threat of its perilous position. Raymond Briggs offers an unusual point of view to heighten his infant's fragile position: we look down on the baby from above the tree; it is swaddled securely in a basket but balanced among thin limbs and surrounded by birds. From far below, a smiling couple look up. Jessie Willcox Smith designs a hand-woven basket for her infant and, unlike most other artists, accents the wind; the sweep of the branches against the night sky pushes the basket off to the right of the picture, as if it might indeed blow away. The baby itself looks perfectly peaceful. Alan Marks' basket also swings from a branch as leaves blow around it, but it could be empty; there is no evidence of a baby inside. This illustrative strategy may be the most complete example of displacement in the images that I include.

Most babies in these illustrations are quite alone—yet another suggestion of their insecure circumstances. But the presence of others in an illustration of this rhyme can also add to the insecurity. Raymond Briggs' smiling couple are thus suspect: did they hang the baby so high in the tree? Are they its parents? Why are they smiling? Anne Anderson's 1926 illustration, collected by Cooper Edens, is unusual in two respects. It shows a startled baby suspended in the air as it tumbles from its falling cradle, blankets and pillow spilling out as well, and in the foreground is a startled girl in pigtails, her hands outstretched—perhaps in surprise, perhaps to catch the baby. Her youth and her ambivalent gesture complicate an already troubling image. Her youth might free the child viewer from the suspicion that a mother would endanger her infant, yet her gesture is not clearly comforting. An adult viewer might recall the times an infant has been left in another's care and the fears and guilt thus raised.

Nicholas Tucker and others have commented on the hostility of mother toward baby in this lullaby as well as in others, and even a brief perusal of lullabies collected by the Opies reveals often overtly angry and threatening words and themes. Tucker speculates that the aggressive words of many lullabies help the beleaguered mother vent her frustration and that the soothing rhythms and sounds, and the gentle holding that usually accompanies the singing or recitation of the rhyme, reassure the infant and the mother herself that she will not act out her aggression (21). An illustration such as Anderson's is similarly ambivalent: the guilty pleasure of actually seeing a baby falling from a tree is coupled with the suggestion that someone is probably there to rescue it, even if we are not.

As the dominant image for "Humpty Dumpty" illustrations is usually an egg-person sitting on a wall, the image most often associated with "Hushabye Baby" is a baby secure in its cradle, sometimes even a swaddled baby. Psychoanalytic folklorist Geza Roheim believed that the tightly bound infants of the Cheyenne and Kwakiutl tribes of Native Americans conveyed their strong superegos—the desire to control their children and prevent wild and roving dispositions (120). His comments lend credence to the notion, cited in Opie, that this rhyme was composed by a Pilgrim youth who went over on the Mayflower and who was influenced by the way the Red Indian hung his birch bark cradle on the branch of a tree (62). As with so many historical explanations of nursery rhymes, this one does nothing to explain the rhyme's long life. The swaddled babies in illustrations of "Hushabye baby," however, may represent our own cultural superego's desire to control our children—for their own protection and to prevent "wild and roving dispositions." It may also be a visual expression of the parental ambivalence toward children evident in this lullaby. The rhyme itself supplies little sense of control except in its meter, and places more emphasis on the rocking and falling—those implied threats to the baby's security. But the illustrations create a balance. They tend to accent a safe baby, a held baby, yet—as these illustrations reveal—a threatened baby. This image must be the most potent and desirable rendition that the artist can create for the rhyme in our culture.

The analogy between dreaming and illustration raises some of the same questions about the links among aesthetic psychoanalytic theories that are raised in psychoanalytic criticism of other visual arts. What, for example, is the source of the pleasure offered to artists by illustrating the rhymes? The challenge of finding new ways to treat familiar material—to ring variations on an old theme—must offer particular pleasure to illustrators just as it did to Claude Monet or to J. S. Bach. But the regressive elements of these well-known rhymes may make them especially attractive to artists. Their primitive content provides artists an opportunity to test their skills at simultaneous revelation and concealment. As Sendak says, the artist must compete with Mother Goose herself (190). Illustrating the rhymes may also provide artists with what Winnicott called regression in service of the ego: a temporary engagement in childlike thoughts or actions which allows the ego time and space to deal with stresses. To Winnicott, such regression was both communication and self-cure (*Maturational* 128).

It is also interesting to speculate about the interplay between an artist's own vision and the publisher's perception of the audience for the work, and how these possibly conflicting demands influence the artists' choices. Jessie Willcox Smith, for example, includes no "Humpty Dumpty" in her otherwise quite extensive rhyme book. Does the omission of this rhyme reveal something about Smith's vision, or does it say more about her publisher's assessment of what would best appeal to her established audience, which associated her with maternal serenity and warmth (Nudelman 38–39)? A quite different kind of illustrator, Charles Addams, was not primarily an artist for children but a contributor to the *New Yorker* of macabre cartoons for adults. His 1967 *Mother Goose* features his own cast of strange characters and settings (now familiar to children from television and films), acting out the rhymes with his trademark mixture of horror and good cheer. His Humpty Dumpty is an egg-shaped little boy who falls from a very high wall on one page; on the next, a small but fierce-looking reptile has emerged from the broken shell, to the dismay of three soldiers. Addams did not attempt an illustration of "Hushabye Baby." Since so much of his work brings unconscious fear into consciousness, and since the overt content of the rhyme suggests the hostility of parents toward children, would an Addams illustration of this rhyme have been entirely too disturbing, for artist as well as the intended audience? It might have undermined the humor implicit in the cartoonists's macabre Addams Family's often middle class suburban values. Is it ironic that most children's nursery rhyme books depict this rhyme, while a book designed ostensibly for adults did not?[2]

Other questions concern the relationship between play and art, and the complex connections among artists, spectators, and art object. Richard Wollheim believes that something very much like displacement happens in the spectator as well as the artist. His recent summary of Freud's attitudes toward art emphasizes the "diversion of attention" that operates when we view an art object. Art is, after all, a form of play, and serious spectators may concentrate on the overt content of a painting to divert themselves from the sense that they are playing. But, Wollheim points out, spectators "may also have to use the element of play to divert [their] attention from the more disturbing or latent content of the work of art" (264).

Nowhere does this diversion operate more clearly than in the illustration of nursery rhymes. Here, artist and spectator are aware that they are playing; the nature of the text being illustrated insures that. The latent content of the rhymes often necessitates this diversion—the condensation and displacement of our attention. Of course, whether any theory holds true for children as well as adults when they view these illustrations is another complicated question which deserves an essay of its own.

We can at least say that most illustrations of rhymes with disturbing latent content, such as "Humpty Dumpty" and "Hushabye baby," reassure artist and spectator alike that healthy people can contemplate their anxieties without losing control of them. Winnicott once defined psychoanalysis as "one big reassurance" and likened it to child care, friendship, the enjoyment of poetry, and cultural pursuits (*Through Pediatrics* 292–94). Nursery rhyme illustration also offers "one big reassurance," in the face of the frequent violence and threat implicit in these strange and fascinating poems.[3]

Notes

1. This rhyme suggests the deliberate risks an infant takes in learning to stand, crawl, and walk. Falling is part of the young child's life. For more psychoanalytic discussion of "Humpty Dumpty" and of "Hushabye Baby," see Rollin, *Cradle and All*, 75–101 passim.

2. Older children enjoy this book, perhaps because it directly addresses some childhood fears. Wee Willie Winkie, for example, is a skeletal figure with a frightening face peering through the children's window at night. "Rain, rain, go away" shows a distressed family floating atop their house in a huge flood, the Statue of Liberty sinking under the waves in the background. And Humpty Dumpty's inner reptile might represent a child's fear of its own primitive nature.

3. I wish to thank Dr. Norman Rosenblood, psychoanalyst and teacher at McMaster University, Toronto, for his suggestions and his thoughtful reading of an early draft of this essay. I also wish to acknowledge the work of Perry Nodelman in illustration. His ideas have influenced my thinking on this topic.

Critical Works Cited

Freud, Sigmund. "The Dream-Work." *Introductory Lectures on Psychoanalysis* (1917). Trans. and ed. James Strachey. New York: Norton, 1966.

Nodelman, Perry. *Words about Pictures*. Athens: University of Georgia Press. 1988.

Nudelman, Edward D. *Jessie Willcox Smith: American Illustrator*. Gretna, LA: Pelican Publishing Co., 1990.

Opie, Iona and Peter. *The Oxford Dictionary of Nursery Rhymes*. Oxford: Oxford University Press, 1951.

Roheim, Geza. *Fire in the Dragon*. Ed. Alan Dundes. Princeton: Princeton University Press, 1992.

Rollin, Lucy. *Cradle and All: A Cultural and Psychoanalytic Study of Nursery Rhymes*. Jackson: University Press of Mississippi, 1992.

Sendak, Maurice. "Mother Goose's Garnishings." In *Children's Literature: Views and Reviews*. Ed. Virginia Haviland. Glenview, IL: Scott, Foresman, 1973.

Tucker, Nicholas. "Lullabies and Child Care: Perspective." In *Opening Texts: Psychoanalysis and the Culture of the Child*. Ed. Joseph H. Smith and William Kerrigan. 17–27. Baltimore: Johns Hopkins University Press, 1985.

Winnicott, D. W. *The Maturational Processes and the Facilitating Environment*. Madison, CT: International University Press, 1965.

_____. *Through Pediatrics to Psycho-Analysis*. New York: Basic Books, 1958.

Wollheim, Richard. "Freud and the Understanding of Art." In *The Cambridge Companion to Freud*. Ed. Jerome Neu. Cambridge: Cambridge University Press, 1991.

Nursery Rhyme Books Cited

Addams, Charles. *The Charles Addams Mother Goose*. New York: Windmill and Dutton, 1961.

Briggs, Raymond. *The Mother Goose Treasury*. New York: Coward, McCann, and Geoghegan, 1966.

de Angeli, Marguerite. *Book of Nursery and Mother Goose Rhymes*. Garden City, NY: Doubleday, 1954.

Edens, Cooper, ed. *The Glorious Mother Goose*. New York: Atheneum, 1988.

Greenaway, Kate. *Mother Goose: The Old Rhymes* (1881). London: Frederick Warne, 1964.

Lobel, Arnold. *The Random House Book of Mother Goose*. New York: Random House, 1986.

Marks, Alan. *Ring-a-Ring o 'Roses and a Ding Dong Bell*. Saxonville, MA: Picture Book Studio, 1991.

Rojankovsky, Feodor. *The Tall Book of Mother Goose*. New York: Harper and Row, 1942.

Smith, Jessie Willcox. *The Jessie Willcox Smith Mother Goose* (1914). New York: Derrydale Books, 1986.

Tripp, Wallace. *Granfa' Grigg Had a Pig*. Boston: Little, Brown, 1976.

Tudor, Tasha. *Mother Goose*. New York: Henry Z. Walck, 1944.

Wright, Blanche Fisher. *The Real Mother Goose*. New York: Checkerboard Press, 1944.

CHAPTER 13

Repression and Rebellion in the Life and Works of Beatrix Potter

Mark I. West

Certain children's authors, such as Lewis Carroll and Hans Christian Andersen, have attracted considerable attention from psychoanalytic critics, but for many years the life and works of Beatrix Potter have received little notice from such critics. Grahame Greene was the only critic to approach Potter from a psychoanalytic perspective during Potter's lifetime. In an essay originally published in 1933 and later reprinted in *The Lost Childhood and Other Essays*, Greene speculated on the relationship between Potter's emotional problems and some of the more disturbing events that take place in several of her books.

Potter came across Greene's essay and resented his probing of her psyche. She fired off a letter to him in which she discounted his argument and then went on to dismiss "the Freudian school of criticism" (Greene 111). After this exchange, sixty years elapsed before another psychoanalytic critic wrote much about Potter. This critic, a psychiatrist named Alexander Grinstein, wrote a biography of Potter titled *The Remarkable Beatrix Potter*, which appeared in 1995.

In the introduction to his book, Grinstein argues that his approach is somewhat different from the approach that Greene had taken in the 1930s. Grinstein suggests that Greene was primarily interested in using psychoanalytic theory to interpret Potter's works. In contrast, Grinstein states that his emphasis is on utilizing "a psychoanalytic approach to provide another dimension for understanding Beatrix Potter" (4).

Grinstein also had sources available to him to which Greene had no access, including the secret journal that Potter began writing when she was fourteen and continued to keep until her early thirties. Potter wrote this journal using her own special code that remained unbroken for decades. In 1958, Leslie Linder finally broke Potter's code, and in 1966 Linder arranged to have Potter's decoded journal published. Thus, whereas Greene could only speculate about Potter's interior life, Grinstein writes with authority about Potter's unhappy childhood, her difficult and prolonged adolescence, and her negative feelings toward her mother and, to a somewhat lesser extent, her father. Grinstein's insights into Potter's childhood and adolescence provide other psychoanalytic critics with information that is helpful when analyzing Potter's classic children's books.

Although Grinstein does not refer to the Swiss psychoanalyst Alice Miller in his biography of Potter, his discussion of Potter's life suggests that Potter followed a pattern very similar to the pattern outlined in Miller's *Prisoners of Childhood*. First published in English in 1981, this book was later reprinted under the title of *The Drama of the Gifted Child*. In this work, Miller examines how children of domineering parents can be affected by this style of parenting.

Miller has revisited this topic in several other books, including *The Untouched Key: Tracing Childhood Trauma in Creativity and Destructiveness* and *Pictures of a Childhood*. By drawing on both Miller's theories about the development of children of domineering parents and on Grinstein's insights into Potter's youth, I have become convinced that Potter experienced a long period of repressed anger toward her parents, especially her mother, punctuated by increasingly successful incidents of rebellion against her parents' authority. This pattern can be seen not only in the events of her life but also in two of her most famous picture books: *The Tale of Peter Rabbit* and *The Tale of Tom Kitten*.

In *Prisoners of Childhood*, Miller focuses on the relationships between domineering parents and their highly intelligent or uniquely talented children. Miller argues that such parents often lead their children to believe that they must excel or risk losing parental approval. According to Miller, these parents attempt to live vicariously through their children, thus forcing their children to carry a weight that they are not emotionally prepared to handle. In such situations, children naturally feel anger toward their parents, but they quickly learn to repress this anger for fear of jeopardizing their relationships with their parents. As these children enter adolescence, their repressed anger often leads to depression.

Miller argues that a "gifted" child from this type of family is usually incapable of directly expressing his or her feelings of anger and depression, but Miller attempts to give voice to such a child's repressed feelings toward his or her parents in the following passage:

> What would have happened if I had appeared before you, bad, ugly, angry, jealous, lazy, dirty, smelly? Where would your love have been then? And I was all these things as well. Does this mean that it was not really me whom you loved, but only what I pretended to be? The well-behaved, reliable, empathic, understanding, and convenient child, who in fact was never a child at all? What became of my childhood? Have I not been cheated out of it? I can never make up for it. From the beginning I have been a little adult. My abilities—were they simply misused? [15]

Having dealt with many patients who experienced the type of childhood described in *Prisoners of Childhood*, Miller has discovered several common ways these people respond to their upbringing as they mature. While still children, such people often take a keen interest in nature. Miller suggests that the pleasure of observing and interacting with nature is something they "could enjoy without hurting" their tenuous relationships with their parents (10).

During adolescence, these children often enter a period of denial concerning their true feelings toward their parents. Instead, they idealize their parents and try desperately to please them by repeatedly demonstrating their ability to succeed. Such a person, Miller writes, "must excel brilliantly in everything he undertakes" (38). If, however, he happens to fail in any of his endeavors, "severe depression is imminent" (38). Unless these people realize that their drive to succeed is tied to their unconscious need to prove themselves worthy of their overly-demanding parents, they spend their lives in an endless pursuit of winning admiration and fighting off depression. Often, Miller goes on to argue, these people are so preoccupied with their own pursuits that they find it difficult to form meaningful relationships with others. Toward the end of her book, Miller suggests that this unhappy pattern can be broken if these people can gain some insight into the true nature of their unhappy childhoods. In order for this to happen, however, these people need to recognize their parents' shortcomings; they need to break away from the idealized and internalized image of their parents and allow the repressed anger they feel toward their parents finally to surface. Miller describes this liberating experience from the perspective of one of her patients:

> When the patient has truly emotionally worked through the his-
> tory of his childhood and thus regained his sense of being alive—
> then the goal of the analysis has been reached.... When the patient,
> in the course of his analysis, has ... learned ... how the whole pro-
> cess of his childhood did manipulate him in his childhood,... he
> will be able to join groups without again becoming helplessly
> dependent or bound [112].

Miller devotes much of *Prisoners of Childhood* to explaining how ther-
apists can help such patients gain insights into the true nature of their
childhoods, but she acknowledges that therapy is not the only way to gain
such insights. She believes that "gifted" people often use their creativity as
a way to deal with psychological problems. As she states in *The Untouched
Key*, "creativity permits survival and helps a person live with psychic damage" (43). Usually, she argues, this use of creativity functions as a form of
sublimation. An artist, for example, may express his repressed rage toward
his parents in a painting, rather than in an act of violence. Occasionally,
however, this use of creativity can lead to a greater sense of self-awareness.

Miller cites herself as an example of a person who used creativity in
this way. Miller's own childhood was similar to the childhoods she describes
in *Prisoners of Childhood,* and she feels that it was through her creative
painting that she first began to understand the truth about her relationship with her domineering mother (*Pictures of Childhood* 3–17). She could
have also cited Beatrix Potter as another person who used her creativity to
break out of the prison of her childhood.

The basic circumstances of Potter's childhood and early adulthood are
outlined in Margaret Lane's *The Tale of Beatrix Potter,* first published in
1946, and more recently in Judy Taylor's *Beatrix Potter: Artist, Storyteller
and Countrywoman,* which came out in 1986. As Lane and Taylor detail in
their biographies, Potter spent most of her childhood sequestered in the
third-floor nursery of her parents' London home. Her parents required her
to stay indoors and out of sight. Shortly after Potter's birth in 1866, her
parents hired a governess to raise her. She was educated at home because
her parents did not approve of the children with whom she might come
into contact at school. Nor did they allow other children to visit because
they feared these children might introduce germs into their house.

Her father, Rupert Potter, had a strong interest in art, and he occasionally took his young daughter to art museums and galleries. He also pur-
chased original artwork for her to enjoy, including a number of pieces by
Randolph Caldecott, the famous illustrator of children's picture books.
Thus, art provided Beatrix with a way to connect with her father. When
she showed an interest in drawing and painting, her father hired a special

tutor to teach her various artistic techniques. Beatrix showed remarkable talent in this area, but her father seldom praised her creations. Nevertheless, she began to think that the way to win her father's approval and establish a sense of self-worth was through artistic achievement.

During Potter's early adulthood, her mother, Helen Potter, made more and more demands on Potter's time. Potter seldom had opportunities to make friends, meet potential suitors, or exercise much independence. Instead, she felt obliged to help supervise the household servants and accompany her parents on their various excursions. Since she had no close friends, her pets became a very important part of her life. She acquired pet rabbits, several mice, and a number of other furry companions. Except for these pets, she had no one to whom she could confide her true feelings. However, her journal and, later, her art work provided her with outlets to begin expressing some of those feelings.

Lane and Taylor both mention that Potter experienced loneliness and depression during her adolescence and early adulthood, but neither of these biographers delves into this aspect of Potter's life. Grinstein, however, devotes much of his biography to analyzing Potter's emotional development. In examining this subject, he refers frequently to the entries in Potter's secret journal. Grinstein argues that a number of these entries provide key information about Potter's "intrapsychic life with all its conflicts and turmoil" (17). Grinstein is especially interested in the entries that deal with Potter's feelings toward her parents and the entries that relate to her long period of depression.

Grinstein begins his discussion of Potter's entries about her parents by tabulating the number of times she refers to each parent in her journal. He reports that there are over one hundred references to Potter's father (17) but only twenty-five to her mother (19). According to Grinstein, Potter's references to her father indicate a sense of ambivalence. She often expressed an admiration for his cultural knowledge while, at the same time, suggesting that she sometimes felt uncomfortable in his presence (18). Potter's references to her mother, Grinstein argues, are much more negative in tone than those that deal with her father. After studying these references, Grinstein concludes that a "thinly veiled hostility toward her mother is especially evident." Grinstein points out that Potter seldom attacked her mother directly in these entries, but she often implied that her mother was manipulative, inconsiderate, or simply tiresome. Another point that Grinstein makes is that Potter generally used detached language when writing about her mother, which, he suggests, helped her contain the anger that she felt toward her mother (19–22).

According to Grinstein's analysis of Potter's journal entries, Potter's period of depression began when she was around sixteen and lasted throughout her twenties. Grinstein notes that her journal entries from this period contain frequent references to her sense of despair about her future. She often described herself as unattractive and held out little hope that she would ever find a husband. She also felt she was a disappointment to her parents. She began one entry, for example, by writing, "I always thought I was born to be a discredit to my parents" (*Journal* 149). In many of her journal entries, she referred to death and occasionally mentioned suicide. After analyzing her journal entries from this period, Grinstein concludes that "Potter's generalized depression, her low self-esteem, and preoccupation with death were outward manifestations of her internal problems and conflicts" (33). Grinstein's analysis indicates that the underlying cause of Potter's depression was the repressed anger she felt toward her parents, especially her mother.

Although Potter communicated a sense of depression in nearly all the journal entries she wrote during her twenties, there were a few notable exceptions. In the spring of 1890, when Potter was twenty-four, she succeeded in selling some of her pictures of anthropomorphic rabbits to a publisher of greeting cards. She received a £6 check for these pictures and a letter encouraging her to send more pictures. As Grinstein notes, the entries that Potter wrote about this development were almost joyful in tone (38–39). For Potter, selling pictures to the greeting card publisher was the first of a series of tentative attempts to break away from her parents' control. Over the next several years, she continued to market her artwork to various printers, and she always took a great deal of satisfaction when she succeeded in making a sale. As she commented in her journal, "It is something to have a little money to spend on books and to look forward to being independent" (*Journal* 411).

Her efforts to win recognition for her own accomplishments also included an ill-fated attempt to start a career in botanical research. She began an intensive study of fungi and eventually prepared a scientific paper titled "On the Germination of Spores of Agaricineae," which she hoped to present before a group of professional botanists during a meeting scheduled to take place on April 1, 1897. The members of this organization, however, did not respond favorably to her paper, nor did they allow her to attend their meeting. This rejection, as Grinstein points out, "must have been terribly disappointing for Beatrix Potter and made her bitterly angry" (43). Although her feelings of depression returned after this experience, she continued to search for some way to build a life independent from her parents.

Her next major endeavor ultimately met with much more success, although it, too, required her to rebound from rejection. She decided to try her hand at writing and illustrating a picture book for children. Seven years earlier she had written a letter to the son of one of her former governesses in which she told the tale of a rebellious young rabbit named Peter. She located this letter and expanded it into a picture book titled *The Tale of Peter Rabbit*. She submitted the book to a number of publishers, but they all rejected it. However, her response to these rejections differed from her response to the rejection she had received at the hands of the botanists. Rather than become completely discouraged, she paid to have 250 copies of the book published, which she distributed to relatives and friends of the family during the Christmas of 1901.

While Potter was making the arrangements to print her book, the Frederick Warne publishing company reconsidered its previous rejection of the book and offered to publish it if Potter would agree to make a number of revisions to the original version. Elated by this news, Potter made the requested revisions, and Warne brought out the book in 1902.

As Grinstein notes, the acceptance of *The Tale of Peter Rabbit* marked a turning point in Potter's relationship with her parents. For the first time in her life she had succeeded in a significant endeavor without any help from her parents, and this gave her the confidence to begin distancing herself from them. An indication of this new attitude can be seen in the letters she sent to her new publisher. When, for example, her father insisted on reviewing the terms of the publication agreement, Potter sent Warne a letter that contains less-than-flattering comments about her father. She wrote, "He is sometimes a little difficult." Then, in what Grinstein interprets as a sort of declaration of independence (46), she added, "I can of course do what I like about the book, being 36" (*Letters* 62).

The tremendous success that greeted *The Tale of Peter Rabbit* helped Potter overcome her depression and self-doubt. Having finally found an outlet for her creativity, she began producing new picture books on a regular basis. Her on-going communications with her publisher provided her with social contacts that had nothing to do with her parents' circle of friends. She developed an especially close relationship with Norman Warne, who served as Potter's editor, and the two frequently corresponded. In July 1905, he proposed to Potter. When Potter informed her parents of the news, they expressed their disapproval of the whole idea. Potter's mother seemed especially set against the marriage. For the first time in her life, however, Beatrix Potter openly defied her parents' wishes and accepted Warne's proposal. Tragically, Warne died a month later. In his discussion of this development, Grinstein writes:

> Norman Warne's death was a terrible shock to Beatrix Potter. We
> can only infer the depth and degree of her love for this man who,
> as far as we know, was her first adult love and the passport by which
> she could leave home forever and be a free woman in her own right.
> As may be expected, she received little sympathy from her parents
> when Norman Warne died [123].

Although Warne's death sent Potter into a period of depression, it was
different from the depression that she had experienced earlier. She felt
heart-broken, but she did not lose her self-confidence or her urge to create.
Nor did she revert to her old tendency of allowing her parents to control
every aspect of her life.

Against her parents' wishes, she invested a good deal of her money into
a working farm located in the Lake District. She bought the farm, called
Hill Top, in November 1905, and the next year she had a new wing built
onto the original farmhouse. Although she reluctantly agreed to her parents' demand that she continue to make their London home her primary
residence, she began spending increasing amounts of time at Hill Top and
came to think of it as her true home.

Potter began using Hill Top as a setting for her children's books while
the renovations to the house were still underway. In the summer of 1906,
she started working on *The Tale of Tom Kitten*, a story about three mischievous kittens who disrupt the prim and proper tea party that their mother,
Mrs. Tabitha Twitchit, is planning. This book, which Warne published in
1907, takes place primarily in the garden at Hill Top, and the illustrations
capture actual scenes of the garden.

In many ways, *The Tale of Tom Kitten* parallels *The Tale of Peter Rabbit*. Both stories feature mother animals who have difficulties dealing with
their troublesome sons. In both stories, the sons disobey their mothers and
are admonished for being rebellious. In one key way, however, the stories
are significantly different. Peter's mother, Mrs. Rabbit, is a stern and unflap-
pable authority figure, while Mrs. Tabitha Twitchit comes across as being
unreasonable and socially pretentious. When one considers the changes
that Potter experienced between the writing of these two books, the differ-
ing portrayals of these mother figures may well shed light on the changing
nature of her relationship with her parents.

In the beginning of *The Tale of Peter Rabbit*, Mrs. Rabbit is pictured
fastening the top button of Peter's jacket. Peter looks as if he is being choked,
and his behavior suggests that he finds his mother's dictates to be a bit stifl-
ing as well. As soon as his mother is out of sight, he heads straight to Mr.
McGregor's garden, the very place she had forbidden him to go. This act

of rebellion, however, nearly results in his death. When he finally returns home at the end of the story, he is exhausted and frightened. Mrs. Rabbit, though, seems more concerned about her son's missing jacket and shoes. She puts him to bed and gives him some medicinal tea, but she does not really comfort him. In the final pages of the story, Peter is pictured isolated from the rest of the family. The conclusion suggests that Peter has learned that it is best not to defy parental authority.

Considering that the plot of *The Tale of Peter Rabbit* first appeared in a letter written in 1893, Peter's predicament at the end of the story is not that much different from the predicament in which Potter found herself at the time she wrote this letter. She was in her mid-twenties at this point in her life. Like Peter, she often resented the parental demands that constricted her life during these years, and like Peter, she harbored a desire to rebel. However, she usually repressed this desire out of a fear of rejection and failure. In a way, Potter shared the sense of isolation and resignation that Peter experiences at the end of the book. According to the story, "Peter was not very well" (56), and according to Grinstein, neither was Potter during this period.

Toward the beginning of *The Tale of Tom Kitten*, Mrs. Tabitha Twitchit, like Mrs. Rabbit, is pictured putting constrictive clothing on her son. In this case, however, the clothes clearly do not fit. Thus, unlike Mrs. Rabbit, Mrs. Tabitha Twitchit seems a bit unreasonable when she persists in buttoning her son's clothes. Once Tom and the other two kittens are finally dressed, the mother sends them out to play in the garden while she prepares for her tea party.

Like Mrs. Rabbit, she gives her children instructions before leaving them alone, but Mrs. Tabitha Twitchit's instructions also seem unreasonable. She tells the kittens, "Now keep your frocks clean, children! You must walk on your hind legs" (22). At first the kittens try to follow their mother's orders, but they find it nearly impossible to walk on their hind legs, and before long they revert back to their natural way of walking. Also, although they do not mean to, they soon ruin and eventually lose their clothing. Toward the end of the story, the mother finds her kittens playing on a stone wall "with no clothes on" (46). She then pulls the kittens off the wall, smacks them, and sends them upstairs. While punishing them, she says, "My friends will arrive in a minute, and you are not fit to be seen; I am affronted" (49).

When her friends arrive, she untruthfully tells them that the kittens are "in bed with the measles" (50). The conclusion of *The Tale of Tom Kitten* differs significantly from the end of Peter's tale. Instead of feeling defeated or contrite, Tom and the other kittens forget their mother's admonitions and spend the afternoon romping in the bedroom.

When contrasted to Mrs. Rabbit, Mrs. Tabitha Twitchit comes across as a more obviously flawed character. The demands that she places on her children are often unreasonable, and her children seem to understand this point. She is also overly concerned about appearances, not above lying, and easily flustered.

Potter's unflattering portrayal of Mrs. Tabitha Twitchit was written at the time she was finally beginning to break away from her own parents. Perhaps her willingness to present a mother figure as being unreasonable and overly demanding grew out of her realization that her own mother was often unreasonable and overly demanding. Perhaps there is a connection between the unrepentant behavior of the kittens at the end of the story and her own impenitence concerning her defiance of her parents' demand that she not become engaged to Norman Warne.

The release of *The Tale of Tom Kitten* coincided with Potter's resolution to make a life for herself in the Lake District. In the final chapter of *The Remarkable Beatrix Potter*, Grinstein discusses this important development:

> During a period of several years following Norman Warne's death, Beatrix Potter gradually entered the next phase of her development. Her attachment to her parents diminished as her attachment to her house at Hill Top and her investment in her farmland increased. The life-style she adopted was that of a countrywoman, a farmer, one far different from what her life had been in London [301].

A key point in Potter's break from her parents occurred in 1913 when she married, against her aged parents' objections, a solicitor from the Lake District named William Heelis. After her marriage, Potter lost interest in writing and illustrating children's books. She devoted her time and attention to her husband and to various agricultural pursuits, such as breeding Herdwick sheep. She also played an important role in the movement to preserve the Lake District's natural beauty and historic buildings. Potter continued to live happily in the Lake District with her husband until her death in 1943.

Admirers of Potter's picture books sometimes wonder why she stopped bringing out new books after her marriage. In the conclusion of his book, Grinstein offers a possible explanation for this development. He suggests that Potter used her picture books as a way "to overcome her anxieties and childhood conflicts" and "work through her unconscious wishes and fantasies" (315). Once she had finally resolved these issues, she no longer felt driven to express herself in this way. In other words, Grinstein maintains that Potter achieved, through the creation of picture books, the same type of liberation that Miller helps her patients achieve through psychotherapy.

Works Cited

Greene, Grahame. *Lost Childhood and Other Essays*. London: Eyre & Spottiswoode, 1951.

Grinstein, Alexander. *The Remarkable Beatrix Potter*. Madison, CT: International Universities Press, 1995.

Lane, Margaret. *The Tale of Beatrix Potter*. London: Frederick Warne, 1946.

Miller, Alice. *Pictures of a Childhood*. New York: Farrar, Straus & Giroux, 1986.

_____. *Prisoners of Childhood*. New York: Basic Books, 1981.

_____. *The Untouched Key: Tracing Childhood Trauma in Creativity and Destructiveness*. New York: Doubleday, 1990.

Potter, Beatrix. *Beatrix Potter's Letters*. Ed. Judy Taylor. London: Frederick Warne, 1989.

_____. *The Journal of Beatrix Potter, 1881–1897*. Ed. Leslie Linder. London: Frederick Warne, 1989.

_____. *The Tale of Peter Rabbit*. London: Frederick Warne, 1987.

_____. *The Tale of Tom Kitten*. London: Frederick Warne, 1987.

Taylor, Judy. *Beatrix Potter: Artist, Storyteller and Countrywoman*. London: Frederick Warne, 1986.

CHAPTER 14

Depictions of
the Mother-Child Dyad
in the Work of Mary Cassatt
and Jessie Willcox Smith

Lucy Rollin

Mary Cassatt and Jessie Willcox Smith became successful painters by focusing on images of mothers tenderly caring for their children—a subject with roots in depictions of the Madonna and child in medieval art and one which remains perennially popular. Both Pennsylvanians, one generation apart (though they never met), the similarities in their work are striking. Smith's most recent biographer, Edward Nudelman, notes that Cassatt's aquatints hung in Smith's home, and that, "more than from any other living artist, Smith's art drew its impulse and sentiment from that of Cassatt" (31).

There are some intriguing differences between their styles, however. While both use large, flat areas of color in the Japanese or poster-like style so popular with other Impressionist painters, Cassatt's images are individuals, portraits, beautiful but not sentimental. Smith's images are idealized, the children well-mannered and well-dressed, the mothers invariably young and beautiful—in short, a sentimentalized view of mother and child. Certainly much of this romantic strain in Smith is attributable to her choice of career; early on she elected to become an illustrator, stayed in

Pennsylvania, and achieved remarkable success in commercial media such as magazine covers, story and book illustrations, and calendar art. She gave the public what it wanted. Cassatt remained in Paris where she participated in the Impressionist movement, receiving awards and holding individual shows but remaining "an artist's artist," not actively seeking public recognition (Roudebush 75).

But these different choices too are attributable to a deeper cause, one that springs from the different circumstances of their family lives—in particular, their relationships with their mothers, and, tangentially, with other women. This essay will explore this aspect of their lives. Of course, psychobiography is a notoriously risky enterprise. Yet it offers a lens through which to contemplate "the nature and limitations of human choice and commitment" (Coltrera, quoted in Zerbe 46). Certainly women's choices and commitments have, as many historical studies suggest, remained limited in similar ways for many years.

Comparing the lives of two women artists from similar backgrounds, with similar training, only a generation apart, who made difficult choices and achieved particular success, yet who responded to their success quite differently, may shed light on those continuing limitations and suggest other, more positive ways of seeing them.

Certainly the tendency in psychological studies of women artists is to find their characteristic rejection of marriage and children pathologic in some way. Phyllis Greenacre's work on women artists (1960) takes the classic Freudian stance, assuming penis envy, the close connection of women's art with their biological functions, and the generally troubled lives of women who do not choose traditional feminine roles. She does, however, acknowledge a strong bisexual component in all artists that makes for their "extraordinary empathetic capacity," and comments further that the more complex oedipal situation of girls leads them to caution—"the forerunner of tact"—and to careful balance and diplomacy, all of which, she avers, restrict the artistic impulse (591).

John Gedo (1983) agrees; though he acknowledges that cultural oppression may be partly responsible for women artists' problems, he locates that oppression directly and only within the family, especially in the relationship to the father. Studies such as these assume that the art of such women is a flawed substitute for the fulfillment that marriage and children would have brought them.

Others, however, viewing women's lives differently, find the empathic capacity of women a source of strength. Object relations psychology shifts the emphasis from the relationship with the father to that with the mother as the chief shaping factor in human relationships. Carol Gilligan's now classic study offers the web as a model of women's relational development: women perceive themselves in relation to others, rather than separate from them. Chodorow referred to this phenomenon, and to the mother-daughter relationship that is its source, as the "reproduction of mothering."

More recently, the work of several women psychologists at the Stone Center, Wellesley, Massachusetts, offers a new model for women's development that acknowledges the "centrality and continuity of relationships throughout women's lives" (Surrey, title page). In this model, the mother's and daughter's close relationship with each other provides a "matrix of emotional connectedness" that empowers both of them and leads to the development of a "self-in-relation," as opposed to the more culturally normative idea of the autonomous self.

Instead of individuation, these writers offer differentiation, a process through which we distinguish ourselves from others while remaining related to them. From this viewpoint, the empathy and tact that Greenacre sees as special qualities of women artists take on more positive connotations, and provide, not a restriction to their art, but the very impulse for it, especially in artists like Cassatt and Smith who take the most basic of human relationships as their subject.

Several studies of Cassatt have been published, but only one with a psychobiographical approach: "Mother and Child: A Psychobiographical Portrait of Mary Cassatt," by Kathryn Zerbe appeared in *Psychoanalytic Review* 74 (1), spring 1987. No psychobiographical studies of Smith have appeared, to the best of my knowledge, and biographical studies of her have tended to be relatively brief introductions to generally adulatory descriptions of her work. My method here will be to follow the order of Zerbe's discussion of Cassatt, but to focus slightly more on Smith, setting biographical material about Smith alongside Zerbe's comments about Cassatt, with psychoanalytic speculations about Smith generally based on object relations psychology.

THEIR EARLY LIVES

Mary Cassatt was born in Pittsburgh in 1844, the youngest daughter of a prosperous family. Her father was a real estate investor, who preferred horseback riding to artistic endeavors. Her mother, however, admired French culture, spoke fluent French, and provided every opportunity for her children's cultural enrichment by guiding them through museums throughout Europe. Indeed Cassatt's mother remained a dominant influence throughout the artist's life. Her other children, Cassatt's siblings, tended to be frail and sickly, several dying quite young. Zerbe speculates that Cassatt's eventual choice of artistic subject—robust and healthy children— results in part from a wish to restore the lost siblings to life and health while "defensively denying any rivalry or hatred toward them" (48).

Jessie Willcox Smith was born nineteen years later, in 1863, in Philadelphia, also the youngest daughter of the family. Her father was a financier and provided a comfortable life for his wife and children, educating his youngest daughter in private elementary schools. Curiously, almost nothing else is known about Smith's parents, not even their death dates. She was sent away from home at age 17 to live with cousins in Cincinnati, for reasons which have never been discovered, and returned home to Philadelphia in 1884 only after she pleaded dissatisfaction with her position as a kindergarten teacher (she supposedly said she was too tall to stoop down to them comfortably) and expressed her desire to attend art school. While her parents undoubtedly paid for her schooling, Smith seems to have felt the need to become financially independent. Quite soon after completing her education, she took a position with the *Ladies' Home Journal* in 1889. Evidently she lived at home only a short time thereafter. Little is known about her siblings, except for a brother who became an invalid and for whom Smith cared in later years.

Unlike Cassatt, Smith's relationship with her family, and her mother in particular, was distant, marked more by absence than by nurturing or even presence. If Cassatt was restoring her lost siblings by painting them, it is certainly possible that Smith was doing the same, perhaps even more intensely trying to restore the relationship with her mother.

The recurrent theme of mothers caring for children is powerful in her art, and indeed, one of Smith's first paintings in this mode is strikingly intense, even erotic. "Mother," from 1903, depicts a young mother kneeling in front of a large armchair, her back to the viewer, embracing her child, who looks up at her but whose face is partially obscured by the mother. The mother's dress is slipping off her shoulder, and the child's hand caresses the shoulder. The embrace of the mother is replicated in the embrace of the wings of the chair, and the decorative fabric of the chair contrasts with the simplicity of the mother's and child's skin and clothing, all creating an especially concentrated image of physical closeness, heightened by our seeing neither face clearly.

It is instructive to compare this painting with one of Cassatt's: "Breakfast in Bed" (1897) depicts a young mother lying in bed cuddling her child and watching as the child eats. While this painting also has a physicality similar to that of Smith's, we see both the mother's and child's faces here, two highly individual portraits. The child looks away, while the mother's eyes examine the child almost suspiciously in a sidewise glance. The effect of these different gazes mitigates the intense physical closeness of the two, suggesting an attempt to distance them even while they are together— something that must have frequently marked Cassatt's life, since her mother was not only available to her but intensely involved with her life.

Nowhere else in Smith's canon is a depiction of mother and child so intense as her 1903 painting, though she painted the subject many times. It is as if she learned to distance herself from her own desire for closeness with her mother, yet continued to explore that desire in many modes— probably a healthy reaction to what was evidently an emotional situation she could not otherwise control.

THE PAINTERS MATURE

In 1877, after terminating her studies at the Pennsylvania Academy of Arts because it was too stuffy and moving to Paris, Cassatt met Edgar Degas, who admired her work and invited her to join the Impressionist movement. He became her master, yet in her words, she could now work with "absolute independence" (Zerbe 49). As Zerbe puts it, her painting became "even more highly libidinalized" as she entered this "tumultuous but intimate relationship" (49).

While there is no evidence to suggest that Degas and Cassatt had an affair, her biographers have noticed that her finest work, especially on the mother-child theme, was done during the times when her relationship with Degas flourished. Zerbe speculates that she thus sublimated her desire for a child by Degas, achieving a "compromise formation: as an artist she asserts her own creative powers, vis-à-vis her art, while defending against any desires to be a mother" (50). Moreover, Zerbe asserts, this psychological situation was exacerbated by her father's withdrawal from his daughter's artistic life while her mother's intense interest in it continued; Cassatt was thus propelled "toward a highly libidinalized and enmeshed relationship with her mother" (51).

When Degas arrived on the scene, inserting himself between mother and daughter, he acted as the "desymbiotizing agent" that her father should have been. Nonetheless, Zerbe suggests, since their relationship was uneven, Cassatt remained in a "developmental arrest at the level of the mother-child dyad," her paintings only partially resolving "her unconscious conflicts regarding her mother" (51–52). Zerbe points out that Cassatt painted two fine portraits of her mother, but never completed a major study of her father (52).

Jessie Willcox Smith also attended the Pennsylvania Academy, found it repressive and stuffy, but graduated in 1888. For a time, despite her successes at the *Ladies' Home Journal*, she then found herself in "a sort of limbo," becoming more publicly visible yet not in the mainstream of professional illustration (Nudelman 20). Determined to pursue a lucrative career, however, she enrolled in the Drexel Institute of Arts in 1897 in order to study under the dean of illustrators, Howard Pyle. "He seemed to wipe away all the cobwebs and confusions" for her (quoted in Mitchell 4). She also admired Pyle because of his ability, which he could evidently teach, to reach imaginatively into the story he was illustrating: "you were bound to get the right composition because you lived these things.... It was simply that he was always mentally projected into his subject" (Quoted in Nudelman 23).

Smith's illustrations too have been admired because of her ability to project herself into her subject; she seems able to understand the intensity of a child's concentration, especially while at play. But in Smith's work, good manners always prevail, possibly reflecting the self-control she must have learned early. And no painting of her parents or siblings has ever come to light.

Thus Smith, like Cassatt, found a male mentor. Unlike Cassatt, however, there is nothing in Smith's history to suggest any kind of erotic relationship between them; Pyle encouraged all his pupils, and particularly sponsored Smith's working relationship with her friend and colleague Violet Oakley by procuring a book contract for an edition of *Evangeline* for them. In 1898, Smith left Drexel and moved in with two other women artists, Jessie H. Dowd and Elizabeth Shippen Green. For the remainder of Smith's life, she would live harmoniously with other women, each pursuing her own career yet giving each other financial and emotional support.

Zerbe cites Greenacre and Chodorow on the peculiar nature of the mother-daughter relationship, marked as it is by "fusion, narcissistic extension, and denial of separateness" (54). Just as Cassatt remained close to her mother physically and emotionally, expressed in her work by mothers and children in tight embraces, visual boundaries were softened and even erased between the two. Degas' encouragement of Cassatt's drawing—i.e. the depiction of boundaries—is further evidence of his desymbiotizing influence, but it was not strong enough, Zerbe suggests, to continue once his physical presence in her life lessened.

In contrast, Smith's work is, on the whole, very strongly drawn, possibly suggesting the clear boundaries that evidently were established between her and her mother early in life. However, Smith's attention to fabric, especially the fabric of the mother's dress in her paintings, which often seems to dominate and encompass the child as it nestles in the texture and pattern, may be a substitute for that blurring of boundaries which characterizes Cassatt, and which Smith denied so early but consciously or unconsciously longed for.

THEIR ARTISTIC DEVELOPMENT

Cassatt's mother died in 1895; for the next five years, Cassatt turned to portrait painting. Then, after 1900, she painted very little, becoming, instead, an active suffragette. Her work during this time reveals a definite waning of her powers. Zerbe comments that such an abrupt change "reflects pathological mourning and the employment of manic defenses ... a disruption of her inner life" (56–57). She suffered frequent bouts of depression, and even explored Spiritualism.

Late in life, living only with a housekeeper and chauffeur, her infrequent visitors found her "blind and lonely, unreasonable and vituperative" (Quoted in Roudebush 89), unable to work or to find solace in friends. Zerbe speculates, "Her tragedy seems to have predominantly centered upon a denial of her own emotional reactions and feelings in search of her mother's love" (57). Since her art "served indispensable adaptive functions" (57), without it she could not act as a whole person. She seemed unable to function without her mother as well.

Smith's later life was quite different. Contracts for work continued steadily, and she seems to have managed them astutely, often making an illustration for a calendar serve as an illustration for a book and thus reaping a double profit from her work. Eventually she became known among her friends and relatives as "the Mint" because of her financial success and her great generosity; one biographer states that at one time she was responsible for the financial support of eleven children—nieces, nephews, and cousins who were without adequate resources (Schnessel 44). Unlike Cassatt, Smith was found by later visitors to be calm, sociable, spiritually at ease, enjoying theater and opera, her gardens, brisk walks, and especially her relationships with her friends Violet Oakley and Elizabeth Shippen Green, with whom she lived.

Another member of their household was Henrietta Cozens, who arrived at the home Smith shared with the others after Smith's invalid brother had died. She took over the household duties, managing the funds and other household affairs—becoming "mother," in short, to the other three women and freeing them from the daily bother of routine matters to concentrate on their art (Schnessel 37). Each July 4, the women honored the occasion with a celebratory dinner and a reading of the Declaration of Independence, "as each woman listened intently. After the reading, the women rose and signed the reprinted document between the names of the founders of our nation" (Schnessel 44).

In 1914, Green married the man to whom she had been engaged for several years. Oakley concentrated her time working on murals in another city, while Smith built a home for herself and Cozens, on a hill just above their first. The routine there was comfortable and pleasant, with Smith as busy as ever, but maintaining her correspondence with her women friends, her portrait painting, and her occasional visits with art students.

This same year, her large edition of Mother Goose rhymes appeared and was immediately successful. One reason for its popularity may be the softer style of the pictures; the dark outlining so typical of Smith's poster style was muted into more tender shapes and textures. If, as Zerbe notes, the intensifying or blurring of boundaries in Cassatt's work reflected her shifting relationship with her mother, this shift in Smith's style may reflect her sense of rediscovered closeness with a mother-like woman who cared for her needs and gave her undemanding companionship.

Another interesting aspect of these Mother Goose pictures is her depiction of all of the characters as young children; Peter Pumpkin-eater is a small boy, with an even smaller girl, out of natural proportion, in the pumpkin-shell. Such illustrations reduce these lusty characters and their odd situations to tender, pretty moments in a child's life. In her calendar art of the same period, she depicted Little Red Riding Hood's wolf as a tiny toy, and the Beast in "Beauty and the Beast" as a sweet-faced, tea-drinking little monkey. These pictures suggest the attitude of a woman who saw life relatively simply and safely, who maintained a measure of child-likeness, yet who had found in herself a measure of security.

It is a question whether she found this security in spite of, or because of, the absence of her biological mother from her life, and the substitution of another female in that position. Her relationship with Cozens suggests that she enjoyed having household duties cared for, yet she also adopted a kind of patriarchal stance in their relationship, assuming the chief finan-cial responsibility for their home. Certainly she continued to mine the image of the mother and child throughout her series of covers for *Good House-keeping* magazine; she continued these popular covers for nearly 17 years, from 1917 until 1934, and they undoubtedly added to this magazine's popu-larity across middle-class and upper-class homes.

As her biographer Schnessel has put it, "Monthly images of children at play and of mother love are not continued out of habit. The magazine's management well understood the appeal her works held for millions of readers" (23). But they must have had an appeal for Smith as well, for they are invariably done with tenderness of texture, gracefulness of design, and expertness of technique, despite their obvious commercial requirements. At this time, she was also in demand as a painter of portraits of upper-class Philadelphia children. No doubt she could have made a handsome living doing this work alone. However, she continued to paint mothers and children, depicting a range of imaginative mother-and-child situations that is quite extraordinary for its variety and its naturalness, as well as for its romance and fantasy.

She must have observed mothers and children closely in life to paint such images, yet the variety of images suggests that though Smith's imagination continually worked this theme, it does not seem to have done so obsessively. And if, like Cassatt's, Smith's art served an adaptive function, she was able, probably because of its commercial success, to continue using it until the end.

Smith died in 1935, upon her return from her first and only trip abroad, leaving her entire estate of original paintings to Henrietta Cozens. In an obituary, the *New York Times* commented, "The children that Miss Smith painted were reflective and a little sedate, and in her art the maternal note predominated. She seemed to be haunted by the vision of two faces, and the face of one was the face of a mother" (Quoted in Schnessel 21). Certainly Smith herself seems to have been "reflective and a little sedate," and Schnessel finds her work, for all its beauty, "in some ways undeniably sad ... [Mother love] is a dominant theme that speaks volumes about her own needs and desires, and this is why her art is so deeply touching" (21).

Schnessel's comments may represent the male biographer's inability to understand a woman who seemed so obviously happy without male companionship. Smith's life and art, as here described, lend credence to the notion that a self-in-relation, developed under initially unencouraging conditions, may flourish later in visual images as well as in a peaceful, fulfilled life.

Certainly, these two artists, only a generation apart, experienced virtually the same social obstacles to their careers. Both made difficult choices, lived with limitations, and let their art speak for them. One sought a way of life that separated her physically from her home and from other women except her mother; the other, already separated physically from her patriarchal home and family (and possibly rejected by them), enmeshed herself in relationships that nourished her and her painting. They were both "haunted by the vision of two faces"—that of mother and child, but their responses to the needs and desires engendered by this vision were quite different, resulting in two different kinds of art equally valuable and equally worthy of further study.

Works Cited

Chodorow, Nancy. *The Reproduction of Mothering*. Berkeley: University of California Press, 1978.
Gedo, John. *Portraits of the Artist*. New York: Guilford Press, 1982.
Gilligan, Carol. *In a Different Voice*. Cambridge: Harvard University Press, 1982.
Greenacre, Phyllis. "Woman as Artist" (1960). In *Emotional Growth, II*. 575–591. New York: International Universities Press, 1971.
Mitchell, Gene. *The Subject Was Children: The Art of Jessie Willcox Smith*. New York: E. P. Dutton, 1979.
Nudelman, Edward D. *Jessie Willcox Smith: American Illustrator*. Grena, LA: Pelican Publishing Co., 1990.
Roudebush, Jay. *Mary Cassatt*. New York: Crown Publishers, 1979.
Schnessel, S. Michael. *Jessie Willcox Smith*. New York: Thomas Y. Crowell, 1977.
Smith, Jessie Willcox, illus. *Mother Goose* (1914). New York: Derrydale Books, 1986.
Surrey, Janet L. "Self-in-Relation: A Theory of Women's Development." *Work in Progress*, 13. Wellesley, MA.: The Stone Center, 1985.
Zerbe, Kathryn J. "Mother and Child: A Psychobiographical Portrait of Mary Cassatt." *Psychoanalytic Review* 74.1 (Spring 1987): 45–61.

CHAPTER 15

Guilt and Shame in Early American Children's Literature

Mark I. West

The superego, according to classical psychoanalytic theory, is not present at birth. Sigmund Freud believed that the child begins life in total ignorance of the moral standards that govern the community into which he or she is born. These standards, Freud maintained, are gradually communicated to the child during the child-rearing process, and eventually "a part of the inhibiting forces of the outer world becomes internalized" (*Moses and Monotheism* 116). With the assimilation of a moral code, the superego comes into being.

In an attempt to systematize Freud's concept of the superego, Calvin S. Hall and Gardner Lindzey found it helpful to divide it into two subsystems, the conscience and the ego-ideal. The conscience consists of the internalized moral standards that come into play when a person determines what is morally bad, whereas the ego-ideal is made up of a person's conceptions of what is morally good (35).

The feelings generated by the conscience and the ego-ideal differ significantly. A sense of guilt accompanies any violation of the conscience. The person feels that he or she has done wrong and deserves punishment. Feelings of shame occur when goals set by the ego-ideal are not achieved. The person feels that he or she has failed and is not deserving of praise or love (Piers and Singer 5–17). Both subsystems are involved in the superego's attempt to control aggressive and sexual impulses.

Although Freud argued that parental authority plays a central role in the formation of the superego, he felt that other forces also enter into this process. Freud underscored this point in *An Outline of Psychoanalysis*:

> The parents' influence naturally includes not merely the personalities of the parents themselves but also the racial, national, and family traditions handed on through them as well as the demands of the immediate social milieu which they represent. In the same way, an individual's superego in the course of his development takes over contributions from later successors and substitutes of his parents, such as teachers, admired figures in public life, or high social ideals [146].

Included among the forces that contribute to the formation of the superego is children's literature. The authors of this type of literature often write with the intention of perpetuating their moral values. Similarly, when adults provide a youngster with a children's book, they may hope that the child will absorb the moral dictates that it contains. Thus, as one of the media through which a community's moral standards are communicated from one generation to the next, children's literature can play an important role in the process of child rearing.

The ways in which children's literature has been used to instill moral values in children have varied considerably over the course of American history. These changes are related to shifts in Americans' views on the nature of childhood. Although the entire American adult population has never embraced a unified set of beliefs about childhood, certain attitudes toward children have gained dominance at certain times. Whenever a dominant set of attitudes toward children has been challenged or replaced, the characteristics of American children's literature have changed. The 1830s witnessed such a change.

The Calvinist notion of infant depravity still had a strong following during the 1830s. Those who believed in this concept upheld the Puritan tradition of crushing the wills of children (McLoughlin 20–33). They placed a heavy emphasis on developing their children's consciences, and consequently their children were made to feel guilty about their natural impulses. At the same time, however, another conception of childhood began to take root. This alternative view was based on a belief in the intrinsic goodness of children. Drawing upon the writings of John Locke, the English philosopher, and Jean Jacques Rousseau, the 18th century French-Swiss moralist, the spokespersons for this view devised child-rearing methods to reinforce and refine the inborn goodness of children (Wishy 21–23; Sommerville 120–135). These adults, in other words, stressed the development of children's ego-ideals. If the children who were raised in accordance with this view did not conform to these high ideals, they were made to feel ashamed.

Children's literature from the 1830s reflected these competing approaches toward child-rearing. This division is exemplified in the writings of two brothers, John S. C. Abbott and Jacob Abbott. Both were well-known Congregational clergymen from new England, and both wrote child-rearing manuals for parents, as well as books for children. Although both attempted to teach morality through their children's books, they did not employ the same methods.

Viewing children as innately sinful, John Abbott felt that children needed to be made aware of the gravity of their sins. This theme ran throughout his most important children's book, *The Child at Home; or The Principles of Filial Duty.* Jacob Abbott, however, believed in the natural goodness of children. He tried to foster this goodness by providing children with an ideal role model in the exemplary character Rollo, about whom he wrote an entire series of children's books.

The Child at Home was published in December 1833, less than a year after the publication of John Abbott's first book, *The Mother at Home.* Both books grew out of lectures he delivered while serving as pastor of the Central Calvinistic Church in Worcester, Massachusetts, and both books enjoyed a large readership. The original publisher of *The Child at Home,* Crocker and Brewster, gave permission to the American Tract Society to republish the book, and it became one of the Society's best sellers.

Like most books published by the American Tract Society, *The Child at Home* closely resembled a collection of sermons. As John Abbott stated in the preface, the book was "intended, not for entertainment, but for solid instruction" (3). Each chapter not only revolved around a moral lesson about such topics as responsibility, obedience, and piety, but also contained numerous supporting anecdotes. Some of the illustrative stories occupied several pages while others consisted of a paragraph or two. Melodramatic in flavor, many of them ended with the inglorious death or imprisonment of a wayward child.

The book contained warnings about numerous sins, including disobedience, deception, ingratitude, and vanity: these sins, though they may grow from infractions as minor as ignoring a parental command, can bring ruin upon a child and his or her family. John Abbott cited as one of his many examples a boy "who began to be disobedient to his parents in little things" (14). Soon the boy started associating with evil companions and decided to run away. He found a job on a ship but, because he disliked taking orders, he became a pirate. When his pirate ship was captured, the boy was brought home and hanged—a fate that caused his parents great anguish. This story, like all the others, ends by arguing that there is no such thing as a minor sin. All are serious; all can have disastrous results.

John Abbott clearly sought to develop children's consciences. He set up a rigid moral code, telling his readers that any deviation from this code deserved punishment. A strong conscience, in his opinion, was necessary in order to avoid a life of sin. In fact, he argued that the conscience should be viewed as a gift from God:

> God has given every person a conscience, which approves that which is right, and condemns that which is wrong. When we do anything wrong, our consciences punish us for it, and we are unhappy.... Every day you feel the power of this conscience approving or condemning what you do. Sometimes a person thinks that if he does wrong, and it is not found out, he will escape punishment. But it is not so. He will be punished whether it is found out or not. Conscience will punish him if no one else does [31–32].

The punishment that John Abbott referred to was, of course, bearing the feelings of guilt that occur when the conscience is transgressed. Throughout his book, he tried to inculcate a sense of guilt in readers. By equating childish misdeeds with heinous crimes, he hoped to make children feel guilty over even their smallest sins. He also attempted to convince children that living with guilt feelings was a terrible burden.

To illustrate this point, he told the story of a boy who played for two hours while he was supposed to be running an errand for his father. When his father asked why he took so long, the boy said that he missed a turn in the road and became lost. Soon thereafter, "a heavy load of conscious guilt rested upon him, destroying all his peace" (34). The once happy boy became so distraught that he could no longer sleep, play, or talk to his parents. Abbott concluded this anecdote by implying that these feelings of guilt would have permanently disrupted the boy's life had he not finally confessed to his sin:

> The guilty child, overwhelmed with confusion and disgrace, burst into tears, and implored his parents' forgiveness. But he was told by his parents that he had sinned, not only against them, but against God. The humble child went to God in penitence and in prayer. He made a full confession of all to his parents, and obtained their forgiveness; and it was not till then that peace of mind was restored [36].

Jacob Abbott shared his brother's desire to provide children with moral and religious instruction, but he felt that his brother placed too much emphasis on telling children how not to behave. Jacob Abbott believed that children's authors should take a less negative approach to the teaching of morality. Thus, when a publisher asked him to write a book for young children, he welcomed the opportunity to apply his theory. In 1835, this book came out under the title of *The Little Scholar Learning to Talk* (later published as *Rollo Learning to Talk*).

The book introduced a young boy named Rollo as well as Rollo's family. Other Rollo books soon followed, including *Rollo Learning to Read* (1835), *Rollo at Play* (1836), *Rollo at Work* (1837), *Rollo at School* (1839), and *Rollo's Vacation* (1839). Jacob Abbott continued to write Rollo books into the 1860s, eventually producing thirty volumes that mentioned Rollo in their titles. The early Rollo books, however, had the widest readership.

Although the Rollo books were fictional, none of them contained a strong story-line. Like other authors of didactic children's literature, Jacob Abbott used his fictional characters to teach factual and moral lessons. He often began his books with introductory remarks, intended for parents, in which he discussed the educational features of his books. The comments that accompanied *Rollo at Play* stated that the book was designed to cultivate "amiable and gentle qualities of the heart" (3). In explaining how he tried to accomplish this goal, he indirectly criticized *The Child at Home*:

> The scenes are laid in quiet and virtuous life, and the character and conduct described are generally with the exception of some of the ordinary exhibitions of childish folly character and conduct to be imitated; for it is generally better, in dealing with children, to allure them to what is right by agreeable pictures of it, than to attempt to drive them to it by repulsive delineations of what is wrong [3].

Unlike the wretched children in John Abbott's *The Child at Home*, Rollo never seriously misbehaves. He generally obeys his parents, often volunteering to help Jonas, the older boy who works for the family. He studies hard in school and tends to learn rapidly. Even while on vacation, he spends part of his time doing math problems. In fact, when Jonas suggests that Rollo stop studying and play instead, Rollo asks for permission to "do two or three more sums" (*Rollo's Vacation* 65). Rollo, in short, is a model child. In creating this character, Jacob Abbott set an example for children to emulate. He hoped that his readers would embrace the virtues embodied by Rollo and apply them in their own lives. Thus, rather than attempt to strengthen children's consciences, Jacob Abbott tried to reinforce their ego-ideals.

Given his interest in developing children's ego-ideals, it is not surprising that Jacob Abbott advocated the use of shame in the discipline of children. While working as a teacher in the 1820s, he often appealed to his students' honor rather than threatening them with punishments (Boles 510). According to one of his sons, Jacob disapproved of corporal punishment. When his own children misbehaved, he tried to reason with them (Lyman Abbott 333–334).

This philosophy pervades the Rollo books. On the few occasions when Rollo misbehaves, his parents never spank him or raise their voices with him. They simply let Rollo know how much he has disappointed them, and then refuse to associate with him until he resumes his angelic ways. Once, for example, while the family is picking berries, Rollo strays away in order to talk with some rough older boys. His father has told him to avoid the boys, but Rollo finds their stories interesting. When, however, the boys steal his berries and knock him down, he calls to his father for help. The father comes, but he gives Rollo the following lecture in place of comfort:

> I warned you against this bad company, and now I perceive you have got into some difficulty with them; but I cannot hear your story about it till we get home. It is your own fault that has brought you into trouble; and now you must not extend your trouble over all our party, and spoil our happiness as you have your own. I must go and put you by yourself, until you are entirely composed and pleasant, and then you may join us again [*Rollo at Play* 175].

By suggesting that Rollo is unfit for his parents' company, Jacob Abbott let his readers know that children who fail to live up to their ego-ideals jeopardize parental approval and bring shame upon themselves.

Although Jacob Abbott's first Rollo book appeared only a little over a year after his brother published *The Child at Home*, the two books belong to separate eras in the history of American children's literature. *The Child at Home* had much in common with the children's books written by the early Puritans. Like such works as *The New England Primer*, John Cotton's *Milk for Babes* and James Janeway's *A Token for Children*, John Abbott's book was steeped in Calvinistic theology. All of these books reflected a belief in the innate sinfulness of children; all were designed to make their readers feel fearful and guilty.

Jacob Abbott's Rollo books broke with the Puritan approach to the writing of children's books. Jacob Abbott not only rejected the concept of infant depravity but also helped introduce the notion of childhood innocence to American children's literature. He certainly was not the first children's author to base a book on this notion; several English authors had written such books during the 1700s. William Blake, for example, published his famous collection of poems, *Songs of Innocence*, in 1789. Nor was Jacob Abbott the first American to embrace the notion of childhood innocence. According to historian Philip Greven, this notion had a fairly strong following among wealthy parents, especially those from the South, during much of the 1700s. Jacob Abbott was, however, the first American to write popular children's books that were based on this notion.

Not long after the publication of the first Rollo books, other Americans began writing children's books that drew on the concept of children's innocence. Some of these books were overtly moralistic, such as Martha Finley's series about Elsie Dinsmore. Other nineteenth-century children's authors, including Louisa May Alcott, Thomas Bailey Aldrich, and Mark Twain, were not as moralistic as Finley, but they still treated childhood as a time of innocence.

During the final third of the nineteenth century, practically all American children's authors, with the exception of those who wrote dime novels, cast their child characters in the mold of the innocent child (MacLeod 151–153; Wishy 81–94). This change had a profound impact on the relationship between children's literature and the psychological development of children. In a sense, most of the child characters in these books functioned as ego-ideals. To the extent that children compared themselves to these characters, they may well have felt inferior or inadequate. Thus, instead of producing feelings of guilt, these books tended to arouse feelings of shame.

Works Cited

Abbott, Jacob. *Rollo at Play.* 1838. New York: Thomas Y. Crowell, 1897.
_____. *Rollo's Vacation.* Boston: William Crosby, 1839.
Abbott, John S. C. *The Child at Home; or The Principles of Filial Duty.* New York: American Tract Society, 1833.
Abbott, Lyman. *Silhouettes of My Contemporaries.* Garden City, NY: Doubleday, Page, 1921.
Boles, John B. "Jacob Abbott and the Rollo Books: New England Culture for Children." *Journal of Popular Culture* 6 (1973): 507–528.
Freud, Sigmund. *Moses and Monotheism.* In vol. 23 of *The Standard Edition of the Complete Psychological Works of Sigmund Freud.* Trans. James Strachey. 24 vols. London: Hogarth Press, 1964.
_____. *An Outline of Psycho-Analysis.* Vol. 23 of *The Standard Edition of the Complete Psychological Works of Sigmund Freud.* Trans. James Strachey. London: Hogarth Press, 1964.
Greven, Philip. *The Protestant Temperament: Patterns of Child-Rearing, Religious Experience, and the Self in Early America.* New York: Alfred A. Knopf, 1977.

Hall, Calvin S., and Gardner Lindzey. *Theories of Personality*. 2nd ed. New York: John Wiley, 1970.

MacLeod, Anne Scott. *A Moral Tale: Children's Fiction and American Culture 1820–1860*. Hamden, CT: Archon Books, 1975.

McLoughlin, William G. "Evangelical Childrearing in the Age of Jackson: Francis Wayland's View on When and How to Subdue the Willfulness of Children." *Journal of Social History* 9 (1975): 20–34.

Piers, Gerhart, and Milton B. Singer. *Shame and Guilt: A Psychoanalytic and a Cultural Study*. Springfield, IL: Charles C. Thomas, 1953.

Sommerville, C. John. *The Rise and Fall of Childhood*. Beverly Hills, CA: Sage Publications, 1982.

Wishy, Bernard. *The Child and the Republic: The Dawn of Modern American Nurture*. Philadelphia: University of Pennsylvania Press, 1968.

CHAPTER 16

The Psychological Roots of Anthony Comstock's Campaign to Censor Children's Dime Novels

Mark I. West

Before Sigmund Freud could write down his revolutionary theories about human psychology, he needed to create a vocabulary that he could use to express his ideas. When coining new terms or redefining existing words, he tended to draw on his extensive knowledge of Western culture and history. Often, for example, he created terms based on the names of characters from Greek mythology or drama, such as Oedipus, Electra, Narcissus, and Eros. Occasionally, however, he turned to the realm of politics for inspiration. Such was the case when he wrote his first major work, *The Interpretation of Dreams*, during the summer of 1899. In this book, he discussed how unconscious desires expressed in dreams are often distorted or repressed by the preconscious or conscious mind. This process reminded him of the way governments sometimes censor writings that they deem threatening. Thus, he decided to borrow the term "censorship" when referring to the process that leads to the distortion or repression of dreams:

> The fact that the phenomena of censorship and of dream-distortion correspond down to their smallest details justifies us in presuming that they are similarly determined. We may therefore

> suppose that dreams are given their shape in individual human beings by the operation of two psychical forces...; and that one of these forces constructs the wish which is expressed by the dream, while the other exercises a censorship upon this dream-wish and, by the use of that censorship, forcibly brings about a distortion in the expression of the wish [177].

Freud was primarily interested in how the individual mind censors its own dreams, but Freud's insights into this internal censorship process have implications that go beyond the distortion and repression of dreams. In *Writing Through Repression: Literature, Censorship, Psychoanalysis*, Michael G. Levine, a contemporary psychoanalytic critic, argues that an author can sometimes respond to censorship pressures by internalizing them. The dictates of the censor thus become incorporated into the author's overall system of psychological repression, affecting the author's writing process in ways of which the author might not be consciously aware. Levine goes on to suggest that in such cases the author's writings can be analyzed in ways that are similar to Freud's analyses of dreams.

Levine explores how Freud's thoughts about psychical censorship can be related to authors who have experienced political censorship, but Levine does not apply Freud's thoughts on this matter to the people who have assumed the role of censor. There are some examples, however, of censors who tend to play out their internal psychological conflicts on a very public stage. These censors not only wrestle with their repressed wishes and desires in their dreams; they attempt to renounce their repressed impulses through public censorship campaigns. In such cases, Freud's insights into psychical censorship can readily be applied to these censors' lives and campaigns.

Key to Freud's argument is the notion that psychical censorship varies in intensity, depending on how repugnant or threatening the wishes of the unconscious seem to the preconscious or conscious mind. The more repugnant the wish, the more vigorously it is censored. Freud argued that this process explains why some dreams are unpleasurable:

> The unpleasurable feeling which thus recurs in dreams does not disprove the existence of a wish. Everyone has wishes that he would prefer not to disclose to other people, wishes that he will not admit even to himself. On the other hand, we are justified in linking the unpleasurable character of all these dreams with the fact of dream-distortion. And we are justified in concluding that these dreams are distorted and the wish-fulfillment contained in them disguised to the point of being unrecognizable precisely owing to the repugnance felt for the topic of the dream or for the wish derived from it and to an intention to repress them [193].

The desire to repress repugnant wishes also plays a role in some censors' attempts to ban certain forms of culture. An example of such a censor is Anthony Comstock. Recognized as the most famous censor in America during the second half of the nineteenth century, Comstock led a national crusade against vice. An examination of his personal life suggests that his censorship activities stemmed from the repugnance that he felt toward his own sexual impulses. This internal conflict not only led him to campaign against pornography, but it also entered into his efforts to ban other forms of popular culture that he found repugnant, such as children's dime novels.

These sensationalistic, blood-and-thunder stories were very popular with children during the late nineteenth century. Known also as story papers or boys' papers, these publications were not well-liked by some adults. Comstock quickly established himself as the most prominent figure among the various critics of dime novels. In several ways, Comstock's campaign to censor dime novels parallels the type of psychical censorship described by Freud.

Comstock's crusading spirit surfaced well before he began his campaign against dime novels. During his teenage years in New Canaan, Connecticut, he developed a preoccupation with religion. Having regularly attended the community's congregational church throughout his childhood, he was very familiar with the Bible and he tended to view it as a factual and incontrovertible document. Biblical teachings about sin were of particular interest to Comstock. He often worried about his own sinful inclinations, and he was not entirely certain his sins would be forgiven. These concerns led him to take an aggressive approach to resisting sin. For example, not long after he allowed himself to be talked into drinking a friend's home-made wine, he broke into the local saloon-keeper's storeroom and spilled all of the kegs of liquor on the floor. Before leaving, he wrote a note to the saloon-keeper in which he told the man that unless the saloon was closed the building would be destroyed.

In 1863, at the age of nineteen, Comstock enlisted in the Union army where he continued his battle against drinking. Shocked that whiskey was included among the rations for each soldier, Comstock attempted to convince his companions not to drink it. After this approach failed, he regularly accepted his share of whiskey and then poured it on the ground in front of the other soldiers. Drinking, however, was not the only sin that concerned Comstock during the war years. Lust, masturbation, and the reading of pornography also worried the young soldier. In the diary that he kept during this period he often confessed to a nameless sin, which, in the opinion of his biographers, was probably masturbation (Broun and Leech 56; Andrist 6). The following entries were typical:

Again tempted and found wanting. Sin, sin. Oh how much peace and happiness is sacrificed on thy altar. Seemed as though Devil had full sway over me today, went right into temptation, and then, Oh such love, Jesus snatched it away out of my reach. How good is he, how sinful am I. I am the chief of sinners, but I should be so miserable and wretched, were it not that God is merciful and may I be forgiven. Glory be to God in the highest.

Oh I deplore my sinful weak nature so much. If I could but live without sin, I should be the happiest soul living: But Sin, that foe that is ever lurking, stealing happiness from me. What a day will it be when that roaring Lion shall be bound and his wanderings cease, then will we have rest, the glorious rest from sin. O hasten ever welcome day, dawn on our souls.

This morning were severely tempted by Satan and after some time in my own weakness I failed [Broun and Leech 55–56].

Comstock was mustered out of the army in 1865, and a few years later he moved to New York City where he found a job in a dry goods store. During this period he continued his obsession with pornography and other manifestations of sexuality which he considered to be sinful. A number of his acquaintances, he discovered, read erotic literature, and he concluded that this reading material was having a demoralizing effect upon them. He felt so strongly about this issue that in 1868 he began a campaign to rid the city of its pornography dealers and publishers. Initially, he encouraged the police to enforce existing laws against pornography, but he soon decided that this approach was inadequate. Comstock felt that most of the city's police officers showed too little enthusiasm for this area of law enforcement and that the federal and state laws dealing with pornography were too lax.

In an effort to correct this situation, he formed an alliance with the leaders of the New York branch of the Young Men's Christian Association (YMCA), and with their backing he traveled to the nation's capital to lobby for a bill that would prohibit producers of obscene materials from using the postal system to distribute their wares. The bill passed, and the Postmaster General asked Comstock to supervise its enforcement, a task which Comstock agreed to perform without pay.

Interpreting his victory in Washington, D.C., as a sign that God wanted him to continue his war against pornography, Comstock returned to New York feeling determined to do everything in his power to make American society conform to his conception of moral purity. For its part, society, caught up in the prudery of the Victorian period, was remarkably obliging. In order to carry out his crusade, Comstock felt that he needed the backing of an effective organization. Thus, with the help of a number of his friends from the YMCA, he formed the New York Society for the Suppression of Vice. The organization was incorporated in May 1873, at which time the New York state legislature gave it the legal authority to conduct criminal investigations and make arrests.

The incorporators of the society asked Comstock to serve as the organization's secretary and chief special agent and offered him a yearly salary. Since this was a full-time position, Comstock severed his connections with the dry goods business and began dedicating nearly all of his waking hours to suppressing vice. During the early years of the organization's existence, Comstock primarily concerned himself with arresting publishers and sellers of pornographic materials, although he also arrested people for performing abortions, selling contraceptives, and running lotteries. He filled the first three annual reports of the society with boasts about how many people he had arrested and how many tons of pornographic books he had confiscated.

Although the suppression of pornography continued to preoccupy Comstock for the rest of his life, his thoughts on censorship, as reflected in the *Fourth Annual Report* of the society, expanded in 1878. He argued that other forms of literature deserved to be condemned along with pornography. Included on his expanded list of objectionable reading materials were children's dime novels. In his first denunciation of dime novels, Comstock grouped atheistic publications, writings by free-love advocates, and dime novels together. All of these types of literature, Comstock maintained, corrupted youth and contributed to anarchy.

The specific charges that he made against dime novels, however, were vague and not as severe as the charges that he brought against pornography. Addressing his readers on the subject of dime novels, he wrote, "It should be observed with deepest concern by all friends of virtue, that some of the so-called boys' papers published in this city are pregnant with mischief" (*Fourth Report* 7).

By 1880, Comstock came to the conclusion that dime novels posed a far greater danger than simply encouraging children to behave mischievously. As his hostility toward dime novels increased, Comstock began devoting a considerable amount of space in the society's annual reports to assaults upon this form of children's literature. The arguments against dime novels that Comstock presented in the annual reports generally fell into two categories.

One of Comstock's most frequently repeated claims was that dime novels had a "demoralizing influence upon the young mind" (*Sixth Report* 6). These stories, he argued, aroused sexual thoughts and created "an appetite for publications of the grosser type" (*Eighth Report* 7). His other main accusation was that dime novels caused children to commit criminal acts. In the *Sixth Annual Report*, for example, he stated:

> These papers are sold everywhere, and at a price that brings them within reach of any child. They are stories of criminal life. The leading characters are youthful criminals, who revel in the haunts of iniquity.... Read before the intellect is quickened or judgment matured sufficient to show the harm of dwelling on these things, they educate our youth in all the odious features of crime.... What is the result? The knife, the dagger and the bludgeon used in the sinks of iniquity, and by hardened criminals, are also found in the schoolroom, the house and the playground of tender youth. Our Court rooms are thronged with infant criminals—with baby felons [6].

In an attempt to substantiate his charge that dime novels bred juvenile delinquents, Comstock filled several pages of the *Sixth Annual Report* with examples of children who he claimed were led astray by reading dime novels. A boy whom Comstock arrested for selling pornography reportedly pointed to a stack of dime novels found in his room and exclaimed, "There, there's the cause of my ruin—that has cursed me and brought me to this" (7). Another case that Comstock related involved a young dime-novel reader who stole money from his employer. After being caught, the boy explained that he had "never thought of doing wrong till he read these stories" (7).

When the time came for Comstock to prepare the society's *Ninth Annual Report*, he characterized dime novels as the primary cause of juvenile delinquency. He based this conclusion on a series of interviews that he conducted with a group of young lawbreakers. These children, Comstock reported, "were unanimous in charging their conduct to the cheap stories of crime" (9), Although these children may have been using dime novels as a convenient excuse for their own misbehavior, Comstock accepted their confessions without question and then offered them as evidence that the "vast majority" of crimes committed by juveniles were "the direct result of evil reading" (9).

By choosing the pages of the society's annual reports to denounce dime novels, Comstock was guaranteed a sympathetic audience, for the only people who read these reports were members of the society and perhaps a few journalists. Comstock decided, however, that his feelings toward dime novels needed to be heard by more than a small group of New Yorkers who were already familiar with his position on children's reading materials. For this reason, he presented his case against dime novels in his second book,

Traps for the Young, which came out in 1883. As Comstock explained in the preface to the book, *Traps for the Young* was "designed to awaken thought upon the subject of Evil Reading, and to expose to the minds of parents, teachers, guardians, and pastors some of the mighty forces for evil that are today exerting a controlling influence over the young" (5).

In *Traps for the Young*, Comstock repeated much of what he had already said about dime novels in the society's annual reports. Rather than make a series of new charges against dime novels, he simply provided page after page of examples of children who were, according to Comstock, ruined by reading this type of material. Comstock did, however, provide one additional reason for banning dime novels. He argued that the sudden successes that blessed the lives of many dime-novel heroes undermined the willingness of children to work:

> What young man will serve an apprenticeship, working early and late, if his mind is filled with the idea that sudden wealth may be acquired by following the hero of the story? In real life, to begin at the foot of the ladder and work up, step by step, is the rule; but in these stories, inexperienced youth with no moral character, take the foremost positions, and by trick and device, knife and revolver, bribery and corruption, carry everything before them, lifting themselves in a few short weeks to positions of ease and affluence [25].

Comstock concluded his chapter on dime novels by asking his readers to join in efforts to suppress this form of literature. He urged everyone who disapproved of dime novels to call for the passage of laws that would prohibit or restrict their publication and distribution. Although Comstock felt that passing such laws was the most desirable way to eliminate dime novels, he argued for the implementation of other methods of combating this "evil" as well. He instructed parents to confiscate and burn all dime novels that their children brought home. He also suggested that parents apply economic pressure against businesses that sold dime novels. "The remedy lies in your hands," he told his readers, "by not patronizing any person who offers these death-traps for sale.... Let your newsdealer feel that, just in proportion as he prunes his stock of that which is vicious, your interest in his welfare increases and your patronage becomes more constant" (42).

In addition to attacking dime novels in his writings, Comstock frequently voiced his objections to these publications in lecture halls. In 1882 alone, according to the society's *Eighth Annual Report*, Comstock addressed fifteen public meetings during which he warned parents not to allow their children to read dime novels. These lectures were delivered in various locations in New York City as well as in several other cities in the state (9).

On February 28, 1882, a reporter from the *New York Times* attended one of these lectures, and his account of it was published in the next day's paper. According to the reporter, Comstock's lecture lasted for two hours and was attended by a "large audience." Comstock, the reporter noted, "was especially severe upon boys' and girls' weekly story papers which assume to be respectable." The reporter also mentioned that Comstock "related many incidents to show that boys and girls had become criminals through reading the stories in these papers" ("Listening" 2).

Comstock's campaign against dime novels had repercussions outside of the state boundaries of New York. Following the successful establishment of the New York Society for the Suppression of Vice, anti-vice societies were founded in Massachusetts, Pennsylvania, Ohio, and several other states. The leaders of these societies paid close attention to Comstock's denouncements of dime novels and often waged their own battles against these publications. In 1885, for example, Boston's Watch and Ward Society convinced the Massachusetts legislature to pass a bill that forbade children from purchasing books and magazines that featured "criminal news, police reports, or accounts of criminal deeds, or pictures and stories of lust or crime" (Boyer 11).

Joseph W. Leeds, a prominent member of the Philadelphia Purity Alliance and a staunch supporter of Comstock, tried to persuade the Pennsylvania legislature to pass a bill that would empower mayors to outlaw the selling of dime novels in their cities. Although this bill did not become law in Pennsylvania, Leeds and Comstock lobbied for the passage of similar bills in state legislatures across the country. Their efforts met with success in California, Connecticut, Maine, New Hampshire, South Carolina, Tennessee, and Washington.

Leeds also expanded upon Comstock's list of alternatives to dime novels. Whereas Comstock simply recommended that children read the Bible, history books, or "some wholesome tale," Leeds compiled a list of "acceptable" children's periodicals and distributed it to the editors of 275 newspapers (Pivar 184). Thus, although Comstock and his supporters did not succeed in forcing the publishers of dime novels out of business, they did manage to make the reading of dime novels by children an issue of public concern.

Any attempt to explain why Comstock thought that dime novels were nearly as objectionable as pornography must take into account his views on human sexuality. From his adolescence onward, sexuality was a source of anxiety for Comstock. He found it impossible to accept sexuality as a natural part of life, but he found it equally impossible to ignore it. Comstock's anxieties about sexuality led him to view it as a serious threat to his own self-concept as well as to the entirety of civilization. In describing this threat, he proclaimed that "there is no force at work in the community more insidious, more constant in its demands, or more powerful and far-reaching than lust" (*Traps for the Young* 132).

Comstock apparently believed that sexuality was the root cause of all criminal and antisocial behavior, for in *Traps for the Young* he repeatedly stated that "lust is the boon companion of all other crimes" (133). Because of this belief, Comstock felt that the suppression of libidinal drives was the key to reducing all forms of crime and undesirable conduct. Consequently, he advised adults that unless they were primarily interested in procreation, they should abstain from all sexually related activities.

Comstock attempted to follow his own advice. There is no indication that he engaged in any sexual activities other than masturbation until his late twenties, and his Civil War diaries suggest that he felt immense guilt whenever he did masturbate. When he finally married, it was to a woman who was more of a mother figure than a lover. At the time of their marriage, she was ten years his senior and in poor health. Within their first year of marriage they had a daughter. But the child died while still in infancy, and they apparently made no effort to have any more children. As much as Comstock wanted to renounce his own sexuality, however, he was unable to banish all sexual thoughts from his mind. In an attempt to deal with this hated part of himself, he projected it upon the devil (O'Higgins and Reede 132–140). Satan, he told himself and his readers, was responsible for the arousal of nearly all sexual feelings.

For Comstock, the devil was not a vague abstraction. He felt he knew the devil well. He constantly referred to Satan in both his private and public writings, and he often claimed to have special insights into the devil's desires and methods. Comstock was aware, though, that not everyone believed in the existence of the devil, and in the final pages of *Traps for the Young* he attempted to accommodate those people who did not share his beliefs about Satan:

> It may not be pleasant to speak of a devil, or of his having a kingdom and power; but I doubt if any man could go through the experiences of my past eleven years and not be thoroughly persuaded that there is one, and that he has numerous agencies actively employed recruiting for his kingdom....
>
> I believe that there is a devil. Those who disagree with me in this may translate my language. All I ask is that they admit the vital

> truth on which I insist. Let my language be considered symbolical,
> provided the evils I denounce are regarded as *diabolical* [239].

Because Comstock associated sexuality with the devil, he tended to think of sexual interests as being unnatural. The fact that most people exhibited such interests only proved, Comstock argued, that the devil possessed tremendous power as a corrupter of souls.

Comstock's acceptance of this line of reasoning led him to argue that human beings begin life uncorrupted. Thus, Comstock felt compelled to champion the concept of childhood innocence. On several occasions he argued that sexuality was not a normal attribute of childhood. God, in Comstock's opinion, did not intend for children to be interested in sex. Indeed, Comstock maintained that when God created children, He meant for them to be innocent of all sinful impulses. Comstock underscored this point by comparing children to a glass of sparkling water:

> Fill a clean, clear glass with water and hold it to the light, and you cannot perceive a single discoloration. It will sparkle like a gem, seeming to rejoice in its purity, and dance in the sunlight, because of its freedom from pollution. So with a child. Its innocence bubbles all over with glee. What is more sweet, fascinating, and beautiful than a pure innocent child? [240]

The greatest challenge facing parents and other adults who cared for children, according to Comstock, was to preserve childhood innocence. This task, he explained, required constant attention because children's mental powers, unlike those of Christian adults, were not strong enough to detect the subtle traps that the devil placed before them. Another factor that made this task even more difficult was that Comstock's devil specialized in corrupting children. In *Traps for the Young*, Comstock provided the following explanation for Satan's special interest in children:

> The world is the devil's hunting-ground, and children are his choicest game. All along their pathway the merciless hunter sets his traps, and they are set with a certainty of a large return. To corrupt a boy or girl, he knows lessens the chance for a pure man or woman. If at the beginning of life the mind and soul be defiled, he reckons that the youth will become in the community a sure agent to drag others down [240–241].

Throughout his career, Comstock maintained that Satan's favorite method of corrupting children was to expose them to pernicious reading materials. Comstock's devil realized, however, that because his pet trap, pornography, was "so libidinous," most adults would not allow children to buy or read it (*Traps* 20). In order to avoid this obstacle, Satan, according to Comstock, had his agents create "a series of new snares of fascinating construction, small and tempting in price, and baited with high-sounding names." These new traps, Comstock went on to explain, comprised "a large variety of half-dime novels, five and ten cent story papers, and low-priced pamphlets for boys and girls" (*Traps* 21).

It was Comstock's contention that Satan attempted to lull parents into believing that dime novels were harmless by not including specific references to sexuality in their pages. Claiming to see through this ploy, Comstock argued that dime novels were filled with accounts of crimes because Satan knew that all crimes involved lust. For this reason, Comstock was certain that after children developed a taste for stories about criminals, they would quickly succumb to other devil-traps, especially pornography. Thus, even though dime novels hardly even mentioned sexuality, they were, in Comstock's mind, little better than pornographic works and therefore deserved his condemnation. In other words, he viewed his campaign against dime novels as a natural extension of his purity crusade. Since this crusade was clearly fueled by his anxieties about sexuality, there can be little doubt that his stand on dime novels was tied to his life-long struggle to suppress his own libidinal drives.

Works Cited

Andrist, Ralph K. "Paladin of Purity." *American Heritage,* October 1973: 6+.

Boyer, Paul S. *Purity in Print: The Vice-Society Movement and Book Censorship in America.* New York: Charles Scribner's Sons, 1968.

Broun, Heywood, and Margaret Leech. *Anthony Comstock: Roundsman of the Lord.* New York: Albert and Charles Boni, 1927.

Comstock, Anthony. *Traps for the Young.* New York: Funk and Wagnalls, 1883.

Freud, Sigmund. *The Interpretation of Dreams.* Trans. James Strachey. New York: Avon Books, 1965.

Levine, Michael G. *Writing Through Repression: Literature, Censorship, Psychoanalysis.* Baltimore: Johns Hopkins University Press, 1994.

"Listening to Mr. Comstock." *New York Times,* 1 March 1882: 2.

New York Society for the Suppression of Vice. *Fourth Annual Report.* New York, 1878.

_____. *Sixth Annual Report.* New York, 1880.

_____. *Eighth Annual Report.* New York, 1882.

_____. *Ninth Annual Report.* New York, 1883.

O'Higgins, Harvey, and Edward H. Reede. *The American Mind in Action.* New York: Harper and Brothers, 1924.

Pivar, David J. *Purity Crusade: Sexual Morality and Social Control, 1869–1900.* Westport, CT: Greenwood Press, 1973.

A BIBLIOGRAPHY

Psychoanalytic
Interpretations of
Children's Literature

Books

Bettelheim, Bruno. *The Uses of Enchantment: The Meaning and Importance of Fairy Tales.* New York: Knopf, 1976.

Cooper, J.C. *Fairy Tales: Allegories of the Inner Life.* Wellingborough: Aquarian Press, 1983.

Franz, Marie-Luise von. *Individuation in Fairy Tales.* Zurich: 1977.

_____. *An Introduction to the Psychology of Fairy Tales.* Irving, TX: 1978.

Gose, Elliott. *Mere Creatures: A Study of Modern Fantasy Tales for Children.* Toronto: University of Toronto Press, 1988.

Greenacre, Phyllis. *Swift and Carroll.* Madison, CT: International Universities Press, 1955.

Grinstein, Alexander. *The Remarkable Beatrix Potter.* Madison, CT: International Universities Press, 1995.

Griswold, Jerry. *Audacious Kids: Coming of Age in America's Classic Children's Book.* New York and Oxford: Oxford University Press, 1992.

Heuscher, Julius E. *A Psychiatric Study of Fairy Tales: Their Origin, Meaning, and Usefulness.* Springfield, IL: Charles C. Thomas, 1963.

Holbrook, David. *The Skeleton in the Wardrobe: C.S. Lewis's Fantasies: A Phenomenological Study.* Bucknell University Press, 1991.

Mieder, Wolfgang. *Kiss of the Snow Queen: Hans Christian Andersen and Man's Redemption by Woman.* Berkeley: University of California Press, 1986.

Rollin, Lucy. *Cradle and All: A Cultural and Psychoanalytic Study of Nursery Rhymes.* Jackson: University of Mississippi Press, 1992.

Rose, Jacqueline. *The Case of Peter Pan, or, The Impossibility of Children's Fiction.* London: Macmillan, 1984.

Rustin, Margaret and Michael. *Narratives of Love and Loss: Studies in Modern Children's Fiction.* London: Verso, 1987.

Stringer, Sharon A. *Conflict and Connection: The Psychology of Young Adult Literature.* Portsmouth, NH: Boynton/Cook, 1997.
Tucker, Nicholas. *The Child and the Book: A Psychological and Literary Exploration.* New York: Cambridge University Press, 1981.

Articles

Almansi, Renato J. "Humpty Dumpty: Some Speculations on the Nursery Rhyme." *American Imago* 43 (1986): 35–49.
Barchilon, Jose and J.S. Kovel. "Huckleberry Finn: A Psychoanalytic Study." *Journal of the American Psychoanalytic Association* 14 (1966): 775–814.
Baum, Alwin L. "Carroll's *Alices*: The Semiotics of Paradox." *American Imago* 34 (1977): 86–108.
Bosmajian, Hamida. "*Charlie and the Chocolate Factory* and Other Excremental Visions," in *The Lion and the Unicorn* 9 (1985): 36–49.
_____. "The Cracked Crucible of *Johnny Tremain*." *Lion and the Unicorn* 13.1 (1989): 53–66.
Bryan, James. "The Psychological Structure of *The Catcher in the Rye*." *PMLA* 89.5 (1974): 1065–74.
Daniels, Steven V. "*The Velveteen Rabbit*: A Kleinian Perspective." *Children's Literature* 18 (1990): 17–30.
DeSantis, Vincent P. "Nursery Rhymes: A Developmental Perspective." *Psychoanalytic Study of the Child* 41 (1986): 601–626.
Egan, Michael. "The Neverland of Id: Barrie, *Peter Pan*, and Freud." *Children's Literature* 10 (1982): 37–55.
Gabriele, Mark. "*Alice in Wonderland*: Problem of Identity—Aggressive Content and Form Control." *American Imago* 39 (1982): 369–390.
Heisig, James W. "Bruno Bettelheim and the Fairy Tale." *Children's Literature* 6 (1977): 81–114.
Helson, Ravenna. "The Psychological Origins of Fantasy for Children in Mid-Victorian England." *Children's Literature* 3 (1974): 66–76.
Krips, Valerie. "Mistaken Identity: Russell Hoban's *Mouse and His Child*." *Children's Literature* 21 (1993): 92–100.
Miner, Madonne M. "Horatio Alger's *Ragged Dick*: Projection, Denial and Double-Dealing." *American Imago* 47 (1990): 233–248.
Mintz, Thomas. "The Psychology of a Nursery Rhyme." *American Imago* 23 (1966): 22–47.
Mitchell, Claudia, and Jacqueline Reid-Walsh. "Mapping the Dark Country: Psychoanalytical Perspective in Young Adult Literature." *Canadian Children's Literature* 72 (1993) 6–23.
Murphy, Ann B. "The Borders of Ethical, Erotic, and Artistic Possibilities in *Little Women*." *Signs* 15 (1990): 562–585.
Palmer, Allen J. "Tom Sawyer: Early Parent Loss." *Bulletin of the Menninger Clinic* 48.2 (1984): 155–169.
Reed, Michael D. "The Female Oedipal Complex in Maurice Sendak's *Outside Over There*." *Children's Literature Association Quarterly* 11 (1986): 176–180.
Rinsley, Donald B. and Elizabeth Bergmann. "Enchantment and Alchemy: The Story of Rumpelstiltskin." *Bulletin of the Menninger Clinic* 47.1 (1983): 1–14.

Rosenman, Stanley. "Cinderella: Family Pathology, Identity-Sculpting and Mate-Selection." *American Imago* 35 (1978): 375–396.

Rosenthal, Lynne. "The Development of Consciousness in Lucy Boston's *The Children of Green Knowe.*" *Children's Literature* 8 (1980): 53–67.

Russell, David L. "Pinocchio and the Child-Hero's Quest." *Children's Literature in Education* 20.4 (1989): 203–213.

Stone, Jennifer. "Pinocchio and Pinocchiology." *American Imago* 51 (1994): 329–342.

Trites, Roberta. "Disney's Sub/Version of Andersen's *The Little Mermaid.*" *Journal of Popular Film and Television* 18.4 (1991): 145–152.

Wilner, Arlene. "'Unlocked by Love': William Steig's Tales of Transformation and Magic." *Children's Literature* 18 (1990): 31–41.

INDEX

Abbott, Jacob 153, 155–56
Abbott, John S.C. 153–54
Addams, Charles 126
Alberghene, Janice 59–60
Alcott, Louisa May 157
Aldrich, Thomas Bailey 157
Alice's Adventures in Wonderland
   (Carroll) 36
Almansi, Renato J. 112–13
American Imago 112
American Tract Society 153
Animism 33

Baetzold, Howard T. 72
Bain, David 34, 39
*Beatrix Potter: Artist, Storyteller and
   Countrywoman* (Taylor) 132
Bernays, Minna 10
Bettelheim, Bruno 14
Beyond the Pleasure Principle (Freud) 5,
   28, 66, 100
The BFG (Dahl) 7
Bibo, Bobette 37
Bombeck, Erma 60
Bosmajian, Hamida 26, 18
Bottomley, Horatio 46
Breuer, Joseph 2–5
Briggs, Raymond 121, 124

Caldecott, Randolph 132
Calvinism 152

Carroll, Lewis 1, 112, 129
Cassatt, Mary 141–150
Censorship 159–69
Charlotte's Web (White) 54–62
The Child at Home (Abbott) 153–56
*Children's Humor: A Psychological Analy-
   sis* (Wolfenstein) 93
Chodorow, Nancy 53–62
Coleridge, Samuel 115
Collodi, Carlo 65–69
Comstock, Anthony 161–69
Coontz, Stephanie 108
Cotton, John 156
Cozens, Henrietta 147–49
Crews, Frederick 5–6, 10–11
Critical Dictionary of Psychoanalysis
   (Rycroft) 11–12

Dahl, Roald 17–22, 91–96
Davis, Robertson 79
de Angeli, Marguerite 122–24
Degas, Edgar 145
Dime novels 157, 161–69
Disney, Walt 31–32, 65–66
Dream Days (Grahame) 46
Dreams 119–27, 159–60
Dundes, Alan 13

Edgeworth, Maria 104–5
Ego psychology 7
Eisenstein, Sergei 34

Erikson, Erik 7–8, 68
Eros 19, 159

Fantasia (Disney) 35
Fiedler, Leslie 75
Finley, Martha 157
Fitzhugh, Louise 23–29, 40
Fliess, Wilhelm 10
France, Anatole 3
Freud, Anna 6–7, 18, 22
Freud, Sigmund 1–7, 9–11, 13, 19–20, 24, 27, 31–34, 36, 41, 45, 66, 79–84, 94–95, 100, 116, 120, 122, 151–52, 159–61
Freud Archives 10

Gay, Peter 10, 14
Gedo, John 142
George's Marvelous Medicine (Dahl) 93–95
Gilligan, Carol 7, 59, 143
Glenn, Jules 75
Goethe, Johann Wolfgang von 3
The Golden Age (Grahame) 46
Grahame, Alastair 45–46
Grahame, Kenneth 45–50
Green, Elizabeth Shippen 147
Green, Peter 46
Greenacre, Phyllis 114–15, 142–43
Greenaway, Kate 111, 123
Greene, Grahame 129–30
Greven, Philip 157
Grinstein, Alexander 129–39
Griswold, Jerry 71

Hall, Calvin S. 151
Hall, G. Stanley 41
Hardy, Oliver 40
Harriet the Spy (Fitzhugh) 23–29, 40
Harris, Bruce 34, 39
Hartmann, Heinz 22
Hawthorne, Nathaniel 3, 6, 10
Heelis, William 138
Hoffmann, E.T.A. 3, 24–25, 75
Holland, Norman 12
Homer 3
Horney, Karen 7
Howe, Julia Ward 97
Humor: Its Origin and Development (McGhee) 92

"Humpty Dumpty," 111–16, 120–23
The Hunting of the Snark (Carroll) 1
"Hushaby Baby," 123, 125

In the Night Kitchen (Sendak) 40, 79, 82–84, 88
The Interpretation of Dreams (Freud) 82, 159–60

Jackson, Kathy 39–40
James and the Giant Peach (Dahl) 17–22
Janeway, James 156
Jarvis, Anna Reeves 97
Jokes and Their Relation to the Unconscious (Freud) 94
Jung, Carl 7
Jungle Book (Kipling) 3

Kafka, Franz 3
Kipling, Rudyard 3
Klein, Melanie 7–8, 18–19
Kohut, Heinz 49
Kris, Ernst 22
Kuznets, Lois R. 46

Landers, Ann 60
Lane, Margaret 132
Lecan, Jacques 8–9, 11, 71, 74–76
Leeds, Joseph W. 166
Levine, Michael G. 160
Linder, Leslie 130
Lindzey, Gardner 151
Little Golden Books 39
Lobel, Arnold 121–22
Locke, John 152
Lonie, Isla 115–16
The Lost Childhood (Greene) 129
Love You Forever (Munsch) 107–9

McGhee, Paul E. 92–93
McHillis, Rod 9
MacLeod, Anne Scott 23–34
Mahler, Margaret 115
The Mail Pilot (Disney) 40
Mark Twain and John Bull (Baetzhold) 72
Marks, Alan 122, 124

Martin, Sarah Catherine 99–100
Matilda (Dahl) 17
Marxist criticism 13
Maslow, Abraham 7
Mason, Bobbie Ann 24, 26
Menninger, Karl 48
Mickey Mouse 31–43
Milk for Babes (Cotton) 156
Miller, Alice 130–32, 139
Miller, Michael J. 22
Milne, A.A. 5
Milton, John 3
Minnie Mouse 32–33
Mitchell, Juliet 7
Moellenhoff, Fritz 34
Morrissey, Thomas 69
Mother Goose rhymes *see* Nursery
  rhymes
Mother Love/Mother Hate (Parker) 107
Mothering: in *Charlotte's Web* 53–62;
  in Jessie Willcox Smith's illustra-
  tions, 141–50; in Mary Cassatt's
  paintings, 141–50; in nursery rhymes,
  97–109
Mother's Day 97–98, 109
Munsch, Robert 107–8

Nancy Drew 23–29
Narcissism 45–50
Narcissism and Character Transformation
  (Schwartz-Salant) 49
Narcissus 48, 75, 159
The Nimble Reader (McGillis) 9
The New England Primer 156
New York Society for the Suppression
  of Vice 163–66
Nudelman, Edward 141
Nursery Rhymes: "Humpty Dumpty,"
  111–16, 120–23; "Hushabye Baby,"
  123, 125; "Old Mother Hubbard,"
  98–109

Oakley, Violet 147
Oedipal complex 13, 84–88
"Old Mother Hubbard," 98–109
On Flirtation (Phillips) 1, 14
Opie, Iona 41, 116, 121, 125
Opie, Peter 41, 116, 121, 125
Outline of Psychoanalysis (Freud) 152
Outside Over There (Sendak) 79, 84–88

Palmer, Robin 38–39
Parker, Rozsika 106–7, 109
Parrish, Maxfield 111
Patton, Michael J. 49
Peanuts (Schultz) 103
Petty, Thomas A. 112
Phillips, Adam 1, 14
Pictures of a Childhood (Miller) 130
Piaget, Jean 7–8
Pinocchio (Collodi) 36, 65–69
Plane Crazy (Disney) 32
Pleasure principle 65–69
The Pooh Perplex (Crews) 5–6, 13
Potter, Beatrix 35–36, 129–39
Potter, Helen 133, 135
Potter, Rupert 132–33, 135
The Prince and the Pauper (Twain)
  71–76
Prisoners of Childhood (Miller) 130–
  33
Psycho-Analysis and Feminism (Mitchell)
  7
"The Purple Jar" (Edgeworth) 104–5
Pyle, Howard 146

Rank, Otto 114
Reader response theory 12
Reality principle 65–69
The Rebel Angels (Davis) 79
Rees, David 91–93, 95
Regression 18–22
The Remarkable Beatrix Potter (Grin-
  stein) 129–30, 133–39
The Reproduction of Mothering
  (Chodorow) 53–62
Restak, Richard M. 47–48
Roheim, Geza 125
Rojankovsky, Feodor 121–22, 124
Rollo at Play (Abbott) 155–56
Rollo at School (Abbott) 155
Rollo at Work (Abbott) 155
Rollo Learning to Read (Abbott) 155
Rollo Learning to Talk (Abbott) 155
Rollo's Vacation (Abbott) 155
Rousseau, Jean Jacques 152
Rycroft, Charles 11–12

"The Sandman" (Hoffmann) 24–25
Sarland, Charles 17
The Scarlet Letter (Hawthorne) 3

Schiller, Johann Christoph Friedrich
von 3
Schnessel, S. Michael 149
Schultz, Charles 103
Schwartz, Murray 8
Schwartz-Salant, Nathan 49
The Secret of the Old Clock 29
The Self Seeker (Restak) 47
Sendak, Maurice 40, 79–88, 121–22,
126
Sexuality: infantile 82–84; repression
of, 159–69
Shakespeare, William 3
Sketches (Twain) 3
Smith, Jessie Willcox 124, 126, 141–50
Sophocles 3
The Sorcerer's Apprentice (Disney) 35
Spence, Donald 4
Splitting 19
Stahl, J.D. 71
Steamboat Willie (Disney) 32
Stokowski, Leopold 35
Stratemeyer syndicate 23
Sullivan, John S. 49
Superego 65, 151–52

The Tale of Beatrix Potter (Lane) 132
The Tale of Peter Rabbit (Potter) 130,
135–37
The Tale of Tom Kitten (Potter) 130,
136–37
The Tale of Two Bad Mice (Potter) 36
Taylor, Judy 132
Thanatos 20
A Token for Children (Janeway) 156
Transitional object 8
Traps for the Young (Comstock) 165–68
Trauma, Growth, and Personality
(Greenacre) 114
The Trauma of Birth (Rank) 114
Tripp, Wallace 122

Tucker, Nicholas 45, 125
Tudor, Tasha 124
Turner, Victor 75
Twain, Mark 3, 71–76, 157
Twins 75
The Twits (Dahl) 17, 91–93
Tylor, Edward 33

Uncanny 24–29, 31–43
The Untouched Key (Miller) 130
The Uses of Enchantment (Bettelheim)
14

Warne, Frederick 135
Warne, Norman 135–36, 138
Where the Wild Things Are (Sendak) 40,
79–84, 88
White, E.B. 54–62
Wilde, Oscar 46, 75
The Wind in the Willows (Grahame) 36,
45–50
Winnicott, D.W. 8, 71–76, 98, 103–7,
109, 114–16, 121, 126–27
Winnie-the-Pooh (Milne) 5, 38
The Witches (Dahl) 17
Wojcik-Andrews, Ian 13
Wolfenstein, Martha 93, 95
Wollheim, Richard 127
Wright, Blanche Fisher 124
Writing Through Repression (Levine) 160
Wunderlich, Richard 69

Young Men's Christian Association
162–63

Zipes, Jack 13
Zerbe, Kathryn 143, 145–47
Zola, Emile 3